Forever
a Parent

Forever a Parent

Relating to Your Adult Children

Carolyn Johnson

ZondervanPublishingHouse
Grand Rapids, Michigan

A Division of HarperCollinsPublishers

Forever a Parent
Copyright © 1992 by Carolyn Johnson

Requests for information should be addressed to:
Zondervan Publishing House
Grand Rapids, Michigan 49530

Library of Congress Cataloging-in-Publication Data

Johnson, Carolyn, 1926–
    Forever a parent : relating to your adult children / Carolyn
Johnson.
        p. cm.
    ISBN 0-310-54451-3 (paper)
    1. Parent and adult child—United States. 2. Intergenerational
relations—United States. I. Title.
HQ755.86.J64   1992
306.874—dc20
                                                          92-15969
                                                             CIP

All case histories are composites—real situations of real people with the details changed enough to protect their privacy.

All Scripture quotations, unless otherwise noted, are taken from the HOLY BIBLE: NEW INTERNATIONAL VERSION® (North American Edition). Copyright © 1973, 1978, 1984 by International Bible Society. Used by permission of Zondervan Publishing House. All rights reserved.

Edited by Evelyn Bence
Cover design by Jack Rogers

Printed in the United States of America

92 93 94 95 96 /   / 5 4 3 2 1

To the adult children in my own life:
our sons and daughters,
who have brought me far more joy than heartaches,
and their chosen spouses,
who have enriched my life.

• Contents •

• Acknowledgments •

With thanks to the many people who have contributed to this project:

Friends, family, and chance acquaintances—parents of adult children and adult children with parents—have answered my questions and shared their stories to help me learn more about parent/adult-child relationships than my personal experience has taught me. They've broadened my perspective and given me clues to guide me and my readers in our quest for harmony between generations.

Fellow scribes Carol, Barbra, Karen, Judy, Janet, and Pat, for their encouragement and support.

Bev, for her special contribution.

My Christian sisters, for their prayers.

My husband, Harry, for his patience.

• Introduction •

The parenting role came upon me suddenly, in a burst, with the appearance of my first-born. I was on fire with a new kind of love, aglow with the ancient instinct that bonds parents and children forever.

With an infant on one arm and an instruction book on the other, the parents of my generation were called to action. There was no question about *how* to parent then—feed when hungry, change when wet, cover when cold, comfort when cranky. Love always. The younger our children, the more clear-cut the rules for parenting.

As our children matured, we discovered that parenting, as we'd known it, had its limits. Somewhere along the line they began to wrest free of the ties that bound them to us. They fought for independence from our benevolent dictatorship, and we fought to maintain control. Peace between generations demanded that we retreat from the front lines of our children's lives.

Our love bond with our young children was based on our protective authority and their dependence. Our parenting instincts served this relationship well.

But as our children make the transition from adolescence to adulthood, we are called to sublimate those instincts and build a new foundation for relationship. It is time for us to retire from *doing* and concentrate instead on *being*. That's parenting grown up. That's parenthood.

Parent/adult-child relationships will always be a potential battlefield. Years after our children have won their adolescent revolution, our inclination to parent—and theirs to resist—may create a minor conflict or trigger a major war.

Change within the family network may disturb the peace. Yet change is inevitable as our children become adults, establish their own homes, and create their own nuclear families. Bonds within some extended families are strong enough and relationships stable enough that changes come naturally and gradually, causing a minimum of concern to any member. But in families where ties are more tenuous or have become frayed over the years, anger and hurt feelings prevail on both sides of the parent-child relationship.

These days middle-aged adults are seeking counseling for the surfacing effects of their traumatic childhoods. They join groups like Adult Children of Alcoholics or Adult Children of Divorce. Most of us (95 percent by some estimates) are adult children of families dysfunctional in one way or another. We are apt to reach midlife before we recognize the source of our own areas of dysfunction. By that time we have effectively passed on our particular hang-ups to the children whose lives we are molding. Given such circumstances, is it any wonder that war between generations is more common than peace? Many of us have done battle with grown sons or daughters and come away nursing our wounds, wondering what happened and how to avoid future hostilities.

We cherish the love bond that began with our child's trusting dependence. We want more than a temporary truce. But we've never been parents of adults before. We're in unfamiliar territory, filled with land mines and booby traps. There is no well-marked path that fits the variety of situations that may arise with each unique child. We must plot our own way through the hazards.

What do our adult children want from us? What do we expect from them? If I knew all the answers I would write a "how-to" book, but I begin this book with more questions than answers. I know the questions I've had along my own uncharted way and I've seen the heartaches of my peers and the frustrations of their adult children. Their stories provide us a deeper look into the sources of friction and the foundations for peace between generations. Come along and explore with me some possible ways of enriching and improving our special relationships with our own adult children.

1

A Necessary Realignment

From Parenting to Parenthood

My friend Ellie pushed through the door of the Mustard Seed and hurried to the corner booth where I waited.

"Sorry I'm late," she said, sliding in beside me. "I've been on the phone with Janet again. I never thought I'd have such a hard time talking to a thirty-year-old daughter."

"No improvement?" I asked, noticing her red-rimmed eyes and the tight lines around her mouth. We'd talked the week before about the recent friction between them.

"No, no improvement. Oh, she called *me* this time, but I could tell by the tone of her voice that it was just a duty call—you know, one of those I'd-better-call-Mom-or-she'll-think-I'm-neglecting-her-again conversations. We've always been so close, but now she keeps me at arm's length. She's really changed this last year."

"Maybe she's just busy. You remember how it was when our kids were the ages of hers. We were run ragged by everything from Cub Scouts to ballet lessons."

"It's more than that. I've wanted to tell you before, but I've hated to face the truth. There have been some clues lately that would explain her attitude—evidence that frightens me so much I haven't wanted to look at it." Ellie's eyes brimmed with tears as she groped in her purse for a handkerchief. "I think Janet and Ryan are into drugs."

"Janet? I can't believe it!" Ellie's daughter had always been such a straight arrow—the all-American high-school-prom-queen type, tops in her class scholastically and as sweet-natured as she was pretty. I would have been a little envious of Ellie's family if it hadn't been for Lucas, a younger son, a hellion on wheels as a teenager. As far as I knew they'd had only one crisis with Janet, when she'd gone off to college in the late sixties and started experimenting with marijuana. There'd been a scene when Ellie and Brad found out about it, but she'd been honest with them and assured them that it was a thing of the past.

"Do you have reason to think they're smoking pot again?" I asked.

"Actually, we're afraid they're into something a lot heavier than pot. Brad and I found some pretty clear evidence the last time we were babysitting. We've been frantic, especially when we think of the children."

"Oh, Ellie, you'll have to confront her!"

"We've tried, but every time we work up the nerve to say something, they put up a wall like you wouldn't believe. They're so cool and distant that they don't give us an opening. And then we begin to think that maybe we're mistaken, that the paraphernalia we found belongs to someone else, that it has something to do with Ryan's job with the probation department."

"Well, maybe it does."

"No, there are other indications. We just have to face it. Face it and do nothing, the books tell us. I've never felt so helpless."

Helpless. A good word for us parents of adult children in trouble. Harry and I were helpless over a son's divorce. My friend Claire was helpless over her daughter's lesbian relationship. Frank, a member of our church, was helpless over his son's involvement with a cult.

Ellie and I had shared the joys and heartaches of parenting for nearly thirty years. We'd laughed and cried over triumphs and traumas, advised and comforted each other in the hard times. In bygone days we'd had some control—less as they got older, of course, but at least we'd had the right and the responsibility to *try* to exert our authority.

"Remember when they were teenagers?" Ellie asked, squeezing lemon into her iced tea. "It was hard enough then, but we had some kind of leverage. We could say things like, 'As long as you're under our roof . . .' or 'If you're going to drive our car . . .' "

"I was thinking along the same lines," I answered. "What do we do now, threaten to cut them out of our wills if they don't shape up? I'm afraid they'd be unimpressed!"

Ellie nodded and managed a wry smile. "I guess we'll start by getting some professional advice. Brad and I have an appointment this afternoon with a drug counselor connected with his company. I'm praying he'll have some ideas for us. Funny, I thought our parenting problems were over when the kids grew up and established their own homes and families. But I sure don't know how to handle this stage. Where are the rules for parenting adult kids?"

Ellie's words echoed in my head long after we parted. Where *were* the rules for parenting adult children? Were we supposed to be parenting at all? God knew I couldn't stop being a parent to my children, whether they were fourteen or forty. But maybe we were supposed to make some kind of transition—a realignment. Parenthood is forever. Parenting, as we've known it, has its limits.

IN THE BEGINNING

Parenting has never come easily to me—not since the day I stood over the ruffled bassinette where my first-born son lay, wet and wide-eyed, reaching his tiny hands toward the dim form that loomed over him, trusting me with his life. I had the good sense to be terrified.

Barely out of my teens and completely inexperienced in the realm of child care, I was overwhelmed with the awesome responsibility for the welfare of another human being. Between night feedings I wandered in restless dreams of misplacing him somewhere or smothering him with too many blankets or dropping him in his bath. In the morning I'd awaken weak with relief at the baby sounds coming from his tiny bed in the corner.

I began my mothering role in the relative security of my parents' home where my young husband and I were living during the post-war housing crunch of the late forties. My mother insisted on hiring a practical nurse for our first week home from the hospital and then Mother was there to help after Nurse Farley left. Other young mothers I knew had had their babies in cold Army hospitals far from home and family, sometimes having to pick up within days of a difficult birth and move to another camp. Baby Kim and I were fortunate and I knew it.

Why, then, was I afraid at the thought of caring for my own child? "He won't break, dearie," Nurse Farley had said with a reassuring pat as she retreated down the stairs and out the front door for the last time. I was not reassured. With echoes of "Watch that soft spot on his little head!" or "Don't forget to support his neck!" I trembled a little every time I lifted my infant into my arms. But how I loved the feel of his tiny warm body nestled in the crook of my arm and how beautiful the soft contour of his little face as he nuzzled at my breast! As joy flooded in, it washed out fear.

Those first weeks were a picture of what the parenting experience has been for me throughout the years. Apprehension. Fear. A sense of inadequacy. Overwhelming joy.

We begin, most of us, without a clear understanding of what *parenting* is all about. If we have an intuitive sense of the magnitude of our role, we wonder at our own fear. The skills of parenting will come automatically, won't they? All kinds of people enter the ranks of parents without a second thought, or so it seems. During the baby boom, when my children were born, *everyone* was doing it—and the faster the better. While the Big War had raged, we'd dreamed of a world returned to normalcy, and starting families somehow anchored us to that dream.

Parenting, in the beginning, took physical stamina and the willingness to suppress our egocentric natures as we put our babies' needs above our own. (Those of us who weren't quite grown up took some giant strides in that direction.) We learned to bathe and powder and feed and burp our small creatures so that they would double their weight in six months and avoid the diaper rash and tummy aches that our baby and child-care books warned us about. Doctor Spock gave us specific guidelines for these practical matters, and I, for one, was grateful for his directions.

Parenting in those days was exhausting but uncomplicated. After the first few weeks, basic requirements for the job were clear-cut and obvious. Helpful handbooks guided us through the trials of teething, chicken pox, and toilet training.

Parenting little ones was relatively simple because we knew what was expected of us. Over time the physical demands of the role diminished and the psychological dimension of parenting broadened. When our children reached puberty, we pushed them toward independence; they responded by pushing us out of our authority roles. Along the way we shifted gears a number of times, but there was always a "stage" that we could identify and by which we could find our place in the parenting department.

A TIME OF TRANSITION

When our own nine children—Harry's five and my four—reached young adulthood, we had good reason to celebrate. Harry and I had blended two families into one and survived the experience. As our children began to leave home, we slipped easily into the final stages of active parenting. Finally there were leftovers in the refrigerator and spaces of time for deeper communication between Harry and me.

Our grown children extended their lives into new places and new relationships, but we were still, for a while, at the center—the heart—of The Family. When they said they were going "home" for the holidays, they were referring to our house. They brought girlfriends and boyfriends to be admired and accepted, and, later, babies to be coddled and adored. When they brought problems, we were ready with moral, and sometimes financial, support. The excitement of their new lives expanded the horizons of our new life.

Gradually, very gradually, both generations backed away from so much togetherness. As our young adults established firm footings on their new ground, their desire for our counsel or approval decreased and their need for privacy and independence increased. That was the way it was supposed to be. We applauded their self-sufficiency. We were ready for some privacy and independence of our own. But we sometimes missed the old days and our accustomed place in their lives.

Harry and I and Ellie and Brad, like many of our peers, are unsure of our roles as parents of adult children. We have withdrawn as graciously as possible from our active parenting responsibilities, but often we're tempted to break into their lives again and help. We watch them taking wrong turns and we yearn to stop them.

Even when our adult children's lives are going smoothly, we are apt to feel displaced. We aren't sure where we belong. We've been upstaged by our sons and daughters-in-law and our grandchildren and a myriad of other people in their lives, and we're left to play out our parenthood role without a script.

So what's a displaced parent to do? Get out the travel brochures and plan that trip we've always wanted to take?

Register for some continuing education classes and catch up with what's happening in the world? Get involved with our church's missionary outreach project? Begin a new hobby? Of course. These things and more. Opportunities for learning, community service, and leisure activity are countless. But these void-filling solutions won't solve every problem for every parent.

ADJUSTING TO THE UNEXPECTED

"We'd love to travel or take some classes," say our friends Joe and Myra. "The trouble is we don't have time or money for any of that since Tina filed for divorce and came home with little Ashley. And talk about confusion over parenting roles! If we try to advise Tina about the divorce or her finances or anything, she turns a deaf ear. She wants us to be doting grandparents, but she doesn't want any interference in her child-raising ideas, which we think are pretty far out. If our parenting days are over, what are we doing with a thirty-six-year-old daughter at home?"

Mary Ann and Jim are separated from their only child by several thousand miles. A monthly telephone call is their only contact. Their career-oriented daughter seems content to go year after year without seeing her parents, although she could easily afford to travel across the country for an occasional reunion.

"With a little encouragement from Sue, we'd find the time and money ourselves to fly back to Maryland for a visit," Jim says, "but she's never urged us to come. She suggested it halfheartedly once, but, when we started making plans, she backed off. That summer just wasn't convenient, she said. Maybe another time. Well, she hasn't brought it up again, and we're not going to." Puzzled about what has happened to his daughter or what she's trying to hide, he concludes, "Sue doesn't seem to want us in her life anymore."

Marcia, a widow in her late fifties, has two unmarried

adult children. Each of them spent a brief period away at college and then returned to live at home. She continues to prepare their meals and do their laundry, as she has since they were born. They are both employed, most of the time, but apathetically unmotivated to get out on their own.

"It would take more money than they care to spend to get set up in apartments of their own, and they can't see why they should leave the comfort and conveniences here. I vacillate between resentment at being taken for granted and gratitude that they apparently like my company," Marcia confides. "I'm locked into this situation. They've never given me a reason to throw them out. Sometimes I'd like more privacy and freedom, but they do a lot for me, and I'd probably be lost without them.

"I'd be more comfortable about our arrangement if other people weren't so quick to pass judgment. My sister thinks it's absurd for the kids to be living here. And, to be honest, I sometimes have a nagging suspicion that she's right. It's not exactly your normal situation. Maybe if I'd raised them differently, they would have left the nest long ago."

AN UNCHARTED COURSE

These examples are extremes in the wide range of complications that arise in parent/adult-child relationships. Joe and Myra are experiencing the "boomerang" effect of children who return to the nest after years of independence. Their relationship with their daughter is very different from Marcia's relationship to her children, who have never really left their childhood home. Mary Ann and Jim are mourning the loss of the bond they once had with Sue, their only child. All of these parents are trying to find a comfortable place in the lives of their adult children.

Because each family pattern develops differently as children grow to adulthood, every parent comes to the empty-nest years as to uncharted territory. There is no established pattern for parenting adult children. What works for one set of parents and their adult children will not work for another.

Chances are, if you are reading this book, you are less than satisfied with the bonds and relationships in your own family. You may be looking for new ways of interacting with your adult children—ways that will be helpful and enriching to both generations.

Before we look to new ways of interacting, let's acknowledge that some of our current relational patterns are usually based on old patterns we observed in our own parents.

HISTORY REPEATS ITSELF

By looking back at our own families of origin, we can usually see a traditional pattern of interaction between generations—part of the established family system. In my own family both sets of grandparents lived on farms in Napa Valley, four hundred miles north of our home in Los Angeles County. Because of distance and limited time, our family traditionally visited our grandparents and other extended family just once a year. Dad would take his vacation late in the summer so that we could make our annual trip to the country at harvest time.

My mother was always thrilled to see her parents and share with them the wonders of her life in the city. She and my father stayed in her old bedroom with the faded wallpaper and the rag rugs. Dad helped my uncles and older cousins with the prune harvest, while Mom joined her mother and sisters in cooking sumptuous meals for the hungry crew. We younger cousins escaped to the cool parlor, where we sat on the floor and played game after game of double solitaire.

At night everyone gathered around the long table, laughing and telling stories about the old days. After supper the men would go out on the porch to smoke their pipes, and my father would forget he was a city banker.

Then once a week Dad gathered us up for a dutiful visit

to his own parents, who frowned on his smoking on their porch and didn't allow cards in the house.

I came away from those years of grandparent visits with a number of impressions:

- Grown women still need to see their mothers.
- Extended family gatherings are like parties, where everyone relaxes and laughs a lot.
- Some relatives (like my paternal grandparents) aren't much fun, but it is our duty to visit them anyway.

Harry grew up in a small Wisconsin town where his grandparents had settled as young immigrants from Scandinavia. Surrounded by cousins, aunts, and uncles who worked and played together, his life as a boy revolved around the extended family within the community. But when the young men went off to war or the young women married and moved across the country, family ties loosened. The folks at home couldn't leave the chores on the farm or spend the seed money to come West for a visit, and the young people were tied down with new babies and budding careers. Harry's family systems of interaction differed greatly from mine.

When we created our own family, we established our own traditions and patterns, which, in turn, have influenced the traditions of our grown children in their individual families. Though some of our children live halfway across the country, we see annual visits as essential. (And we have no farm chores to tie us to our "acre.")

Although circumstances and tradition help shape our patterns of interaction with our adult children, we are not always satisfied with the results.

"I've watched our next-door neighbors with more than a little envy," Sheila confessed. "Ed and I sit in our own patio alone on Sunday afternoons, listening to the sounds of their happy family gatherings—three generations enjoying one another. Grandfather and grandson shooting baskets in the driveway. Grandma and the rest of the women laughing together as they bring out platters of food for their traditional after-church picnic. Sometimes they look over the fence and invite us to join them, and then we suspect they're feeling sorry for us. They know our three kids live within twenty miles of here, and I'm sure they wonder why they don't come over more.

"We used to see more of them when their children were little, but things have changed in the last few years. We got to thinking that maybe we hadn't encouraged them to drop in, but when we tried, it just didn't work out. They're busy with so many things. We get together for an annual family reunion in the summer when my sister Betsy comes out from Iowa, and everyone seems to enjoy that. But I'd like our kids to be more involved with us on a regular basis."

As she considered the model she and Ed had demonstrated to their children, Sheila gained new insight. "It's no wonder they don't come around more," she said. "We didn't go out of our way to visit my folks or Ed's between birthdays and holidays. There were enough of those to keep us in pretty close touch, and between occasions we were busy with our own family projects. Our neighbors come from a different culture, and I have no business comparing lifestyles. We have good relationships with all of our children, and I think that's what counts."

A NEW ROLE

Though our active parenting years pass quickly, we face many years ahead of adult-to-adult relationships with our children. Each generation has much to offer the others, and we are missing out if we don't work toward relationships that enrich all of our lives. If we feel displaced by our children's maturity and independence, it's because we can't fit into their lives in the same way that we did when they were youngsters. But we can find a new place and a new way of fitting.

The maternal or paternal love that took root in our hearts in those first hours of parenthood is there to stay. In the beginning that love is readily channeled into nurturing and guiding. That was God's plan for parents. When our children are grown, ready or not, those nurturing and guiding years are over. If we would stay in their lives, we need to take on a new role, to channel our love in a new way.

As parents of adult children our roles are not well-defined. Your role will be different from mine and will probably be different with each of your children. (I've found that my place in a daughter's life is very different from that in a son's.) The challenge for each of us is to seek ways of channeling our parental love in the direction of their grown-up needs, without discounting our own needs.

QUESTIONS FOR YOU

1. Can you identify with Ellie's frustration over her daughter's situation?

2. What would you do under similar circumstances?

3. What difficulties or frustrations do you have in your dealings with your adult children?

4. In what ways is your role the same or different with each of your grown children?

5. In what ways do you want your relationship with your adult child to be similar to or different from your relationship with your parent?

6. How do you see your role as the parent of adult children?

2

Declaration of War
The Adolescent Revolution

Most of my peers are parents of those post-World-War-II baby boomers who make up the largest segment of our population. We joyfully brought them into a battle-weary world to prove our faith in a warless future. We did our best, most of us, to nurture and guide them into adults capable of maintaining our peace-and-prosperity world—to do what our parents had failed to do for us. We were young and idealistic. Then, when our children grew up to burn draft cards and march in protest of war, we accused *them* of being young and idealistic. In spite of our dreams and their protests, peace in our world has fallen short of anyone's ideal. So, too often, has peace between generations.

THE REVOLUTION

Conflict between parent and child begins in earnest at puberty, if not before. Rebellion—pushing away from parental control—is a natural and necessary process of maturity. Some of us engage in all-out battle with our adolescent children; others experience only an occasional skirmish or a few months of cold war. No matter how carefree and trusting the former parent-child relationships, we become the enemy.

Growing up is a scary prospect. No matter how confident—or arrogant—adolescents appear to their parents, underneath they are confused and unsettled by the physical and emotional changes going on in their minds and bodies. The more insecure they feel, the more apt they are to lash out at the parents who have always protected them and now seem oblivious to their misery.

Rewind your memory tape. Remember your own bewildering days of budding breast or cracking voice and parents who failed to understand the manic-depressive emotions that confused and controlled you? You probably didn't like your parents much in those days, and chances are you weren't too loveable yourself. Hostilities erupted at the least provocation. Remember? Now fast-forward your tape to the time when your children were fighting their own battles for independence. In spite of your experience, weren't you surprised when fourteen-year-old Susie stood toe-to-toe with you and defied your authority? Shocked and hurt at her sudden lack of respect? Somewhere, when you weren't looking, the space between you and your child had widened and become a war zone.

Having the benefits of our own youthful experience plus a superabundance of professional guidelines for surviving our children's adolescence, you would think we would be better prepared for the inevitable conflict. But somehow we are always surprised at *our* beloved child and his betrayal of the love-bond we have shared. Defensive and hurt, we strike back with whatever weapons we can muster.

Jay Kesler, author of *Ten Mistakes Parents Make with Teenagers (And How to Avoid Them)*, says,

> One of the great principles of parenting comes from Newton's Law: *For each action there is an equal and opposite reaction.* If parents don't react strongly to everything their teenagers do, then teenagers won't act out contrary behavior with such enthusiasm.[1]

If only we would take this author's advice! But we are driven by our God-given protective instinct, by fear of the consequences of our child's actions, by hurt turned to anger at a suddenly changed relationship, and by pride that wants to see our child as the shining product of exemplary parenting. So our adolescent's rebellious *action* provokes a "strong" parental *reaction* born of fear, hurt, and pride, which in turn provokes zealous "contrary behavior." And the war is on!

Our weapons range from the guilt-producing "After all I've done for you," to the triumphant "You're grounded!" Children retaliate with barbs of their own: "You're too busy at your precious office to know what's going on in my life! Nobody cares about my feelings!" With battle lines drawn, the two generations move into open combat. Love is submerged beneath tempers and tears.

WOUNDS OF WAR

Every war has its casualties. If parents do not make the effort to negotiate a peace, serious wounds will result that may damage the family unit beyond repair. This is what happened to successful businessman Don Wright:

"I grew up in a strict religious community where the church leaders had too much to say about each family's business. They overruled the parents in deciding the future direction of each child. The church leaders decided who would be apprenticed to whom to learn which trade and who would have the privilege of going on to higher education. When I was thirteen years old and just finishing the eighth grade, these officials decided that I should leave school and train as a carpenter.

"I was devastated, angry, and rebellious. I had looked forward with great enthusiasm to high school and dreamed of earning a scholarship to college. My teacher, who was part of the same community but less rigid in his outlook, had encouraged me. My grades were superior; there was no reason for me to be chosen for a future of manual labor, except that I had worked with my uncle the summer before, remodeling our church. I pleaded with my dad and begged my mother to intervene, but it was useless. From my dad's point of view, my defiance was grounds for stricter discipline. From my perspective, he was grossly unfair.

"After a violent quarrel, in which bitter words were hurled back and forth like daggers, leaving permanent scars upon the hearts of all of us, I left home to live with another family. These kind people sympathized with my plight and were willing to give me board and room during my high-school years. I worked on their farm and at odd jobs in town until I graduated. I did well enough in school to earn a full scholarship to a good university.

"I've never regretted fighting for my right to an education, but I'm deeply sorry that I had to sever my family ties in the process. The experience also threatened my faith, as it was a long time before I could differentiate between true Christianity and the religious legalism of my childhood.

"I managed to visit my mother a few times during those growing-up years, but I didn't see my father again until a few months before he died. When we met, we were like strangers. I thought maybe he would apologize—I guess I expected it—but he never even mentioned our long separation. It was too late to resolve our ancient feud, and without resolution of what had separated us, there could be no real relationship. An armed truce was the closest we ever came to peace between us."

What a sad story! A stubborn, hard-hearted father, reacting too strongly to his son's understandable rebellion, sacrificed a potentially rich father-son relationship to his rigid principles. When his son left home, the doors slammed behind him. The father's inability to compromise caused injuries that destroyed a family.

Probably, like most parents, he was trying to do what he

thought was right. If he could have been guided instead by the biblical admonition, "Fathers, do not embitter your children, or they will become discouraged" (Col. 3:21), how different the outcome might have been.

WHEAT AND TARES

"A man reaps what he sows," warns Paul in Galatians 6:7. Throughout the Bible we read a lot about sowing and reaping. Adolescence is a fertile field for seeds of dissension. Anger and bitterness sown and cultivated at that sensitive time can produce a harvest of misunderstanding and resentment in future years. Fortunately, most parents don't reap such extreme consequences as Don Wright's father, but all parents sow seeds that will appear as wheat or tares in their future relationship with their adult children.

My friend Doreen shared an experience from her teen years. "During my senior year in high school, a girlfriend and I cut school to go to Santa Barbara in her car. Of course we were breaking all kinds of rules—like she wasn't supposed to drive that far—but cutting school was a pretty common practice and neither of us had ever done it before. We were both good students and generally good kids—not wild like some of the senior girls. We picked up a couple of boys at the mall and went over to this guy's house—dumb, I admit— and played old records and smoked cigarettes and drank a little beer. I think we girls split one can between us, because we knew we had to drive home. We got home at our usual times and no one would have known the difference except for this blabbermouth kid who saw us driving down State Street and reported us to the principal. She called my mother, who trusted me implicitly and didn't want to believe a word of the story.

"Even though I'd done something wrong, I hadn't been feeling particularly guilty. We hadn't committed any grave sin. But when Mom confronted me with the principal's accusation, I realized how I'd let her down. I denied it, which was a dumb move on my part; I was a poor liar. But I stuck to my denial, and Mom was confused enough to snoop around in my room until she found my diary with the written account of our clandestine adventure. She was crushed because I'd deceived her, and I was furious because she'd invaded my privacy. The whole episode was a blight on our relationship. I think it took years for us to begin to trust each other again."

Doreen's mother told me how that particular experience affected her. "I was more hurt than anything," she said. "Doreen had always been so open with me, and I couldn't believe she'd do something like that. Then, when I had the proof in front of me, my imagination went crazy and I suspected her of all sorts of things. I felt like a thief looking through her diary, and I wish now I'd never done it, but somehow I *had* to know what kind of woman my daughter was becoming. I didn't find any more incriminating evidence of misconduct, but I couldn't get over my hurt and distrust. Doreen and I are pretty good friends now, and she has a sixteen-year-old of her own, so maybe she understands a little. I think I have a more realistic perspective of my granddaughter than I had of her mother. Even so, I look back on that particular episode as a divisive one in our relationship. The hurt to both of us has never quite healed."

Many of us in both generations can identify with Doreen's story. The adolescent's inevitable quest for privacy often leads to uncharacteristic deceit. The parent finds herself on unfamiliar ground and reacts badly.

Even if damage to the parent-child bond is minimal, it is likely to surface a couple of decades hence. At thirty-five I found myself looking back at an episode between my mother and me—she had humiliated me in front of my friends—and began to resent her all over again. Why then? Perhaps because I was going through a difficult time with my own daughter and looking for food for self-pity. As Doreen's mother said, some hurts never quite heal.

THE SCARS OF ABUSE

The rebellious acts and emotional outbursts typical of adolescence sometimes trigger physical and psychological abuse from formerly nonabusive parents. One father lost control of his temper when he began to lose control of his teenager.

"My dad didn't start knocking me around until I was seventeen," said Erik. "That was about the time I decided I'd had enough of his dictatorship. He wanted to pick my friends, my summer jobs, even my electives in school. You couldn't argue with him, because he was always right about everything. I just said 'Yes sir' and went ahead and did my own thing. When he found out I'd taken a job he hadn't okayed, he went crazy and started slugging me. I was a pretty big kid for my age, so I could have put him down with one hand, but my mom and sister were standing there crying, so I just tried to defend myself until I could walk away from him. How is a guy supposed to fight his own father? From then on, anything I did that was contrary to his wishes was an excuse for him to pound on me."

When Erik's father could no longer control his son by dictating his every move, he panicked. His home was the one area of his life where he had always been king, and his ego was crushed at Erik's rebellion. He reacted in rage and his kingdom became a battleground. In attempting to maintain his iron-fist rule, Erik's father forfeited any chance he might have had to influence and guide his son as he grew into adulthood.

"There were things about my dad I respected," Erik said. "If we'd been able to have a normal conversation, I would have gone to him for advice sometimes. But with him there was no such thing as advice. He gave orders, not advice.

"I left home the day after I graduated from high school, and I don't go back very often. When I do, I keep Dad at arm's length, literally and figuratively. I wouldn't think of consulting him about any decision I have to make—with him it's total control or nothing. I envy my friend Tom, who can talk to his dad about almost anything without risking an explosion. Oh, I don't suppose Dad would get physical with me any more, but his verbal abuse can be almost as bad."

Erik's abuse was rooted in his father's fear. There is at least a kernel of fear in all of us when we realize that we can no longer force our children to do the things that are good for them or prevent them from behavior that will hurt them. Erik's father's fear was compounded by his poor self-image. He relied upon his family's unquestioning obedience to support his fragile ego. Had he approached his son's adolescence more realistically, acknowledging the inevitability of change and independence, he could have avoided some of the frustration and conflict that left scars on the father-son relationship.

A PARENT'S AMBITION

Some parents unconsciously try to fulfill their own lost dreams through their children by directing them down wrong paths—not necessarily wrong in accordance with God's principles, but wrong for that child's personality type.

Proverbs 22:6 tells us to "train a child in the way he should go," a directive that can be wrongly interpreted to mean "according to his parents' values." The intent of the original Hebrew is more like "train a child according to his bent"—according to his or her individual and unique disposition, abilities, and talents.

A parent who projects personal ambitions on an adolescent son or daughter without regard for that child's "bent" will widen the natural breach between them and reduce the chances for a satisfactory future relationship with the child as an adult. In an ideal situation, a parent is sensitive to each child's uniqueness. As the facets of the child's personality take shape, the parent is there to guide her toward fulfillment of her special potential. If a parent is so intent on a personal agenda that he or she discounts a child's inclinations, the child will feel discounted, even if the feelings aren't identified as such.

Allen, an attorney who spends more time at his hobby of furniture-making than is good for his practice, says, "I have no desire to be a big-time attorney like my dad. To be honest, I wouldn't have gone to law school at all if I'd had the courage to stand up to Dad. I loved to build things and was pretty good at it—got a blue ribbon at the fair for a table I designed and made from scratch. But when I told my dad that's what I wanted to do for a living, he just laughed. 'You can take up a hobby when you get enough money coming in to afford it,' he said. 'You better quit playing around and make something of yourself.' I did what he expected, but it was his ambition for me, not mine. Our local high school is looking for a wood-shop teacher, and for two cents I'd chuck the law career and go for it. My dad and I don't get along that well anyway, so what would I have to lose besides a lot of headaches?"

Allen's dad had belittled his son's dream and the hurt lived on. Perhaps Allen eventually saw a way to retaliate for the hurt by chucking his law career for a job closer to his heart.

WHEN LIFE OVERWHELMS

Our relationships with our children build gradually over the years. From the bonding of infancy to the wrenching separation at adolescence, times of closeness between parent and child are interspersed with periods of conflict. Each age and stage is a new challenge to be met with whatever strengths or abilities we can call forth at that particular time.

Even as we strive for consistency in our parenting, our coping abilities ebb and flow with the tide of circumstances.

A parent who is chronically ill, threatened with bankruptcy, or facing divorce may be incapable of effective parenting. When an adult crisis coincides with the inevitable crisis of adolescent rebellion, the child may feel deserted, emotionally or physically. How damaging this will be to the ongoing parent-child relationship depends upon several factors: the quality of the relationship achieved during the child's preadolescent years, the degree of the child's emotional dependency when the crisis hits, and the duration of the crisis period.

Some years ago Harry and I were involved in a prerelease program at a nearby federal prison. Most of the inmates with whom we had contact were young men in their twenties—the ages of our own sons—who had been incarcerated for drug-related crimes. Without their prison garb, they could easily have blended into the student population of our local college. They were enthusiastic, polite, and grateful for our interest. My maternal heart went out to each of them as we became acquainted during our bimonthly visits. We asked questions and they responded, telling us of childhood memories, dreams, and disappointments. One common thread seemed to run through their stories: parents who had let them down.

- "My stepfather locked me out of the house when I was fourteen."
- "My dad came back from the war with mental problems—spent months at a time at the veteran's hospital. My mom drank."
- "My mother died of cancer when I was fifteen, and my dad married a lady who didn't like kids."
- "I was doing okay until my dad lost his job and we moved to a lousy part of town. In East L.A. you had to join a gang to survive."

Story after story told of parents who, because of some

crisis of their own, had turned the course of a son's life. A young man spending the prime years of his life in prison can be forgiven for placing blame upon the adults who had failed him, for whatever reason. "If my dad hadn't married that witch . . ." "If we'd stayed in the old neighborhood . . ."

We came to know twenty-year-old Mike rather well. His father had been physically and psychologically wounded by war, rendered incapable of parenting the son he'd conceived between boot camp and battle; his mother, robbed of the dreams that sustained her while she waited for her soldier husband to come home, turned to alcohol for comfort. Mike, left to fend for himself, took up with the wrong crowd. He blamed his parents for their lack of support during his troubled teens. By the time Mike was paroled from prison his father was dead and his mother was sober. Though he was apprehensive about going home, he and his mother were drawn to each other in their mutual need. They managed to establish a warm relationship before his mother was killed in an automobile accident. "We've had some long talks," he wrote. "I've finally been able to see my parents as people and understand a little of what happened to them."

Although Mike had a lot to battle in "making it on the outside," he had a better chance for success after he'd overcome some of his resentment toward his parents and their emotional absence in his teens.

Harlan, the young man whose stepfather locked him out of the house, was not so fortunate. Having spent most of his teen years as a ward of the state, he was bitter. "They used to try to involve my parents when I got caught for burglary or something, but my real dad was long gone and my stepdad wanted no part of me. He and my mother got me declared incorrigible and washed their hands of the whole mess. They could just as well be dead now for all I care." When Harlan left prison, he carried an extra burden of resentment. Without a place to go or a family to care, he was likely to return to prison. The last we heard, he had been arrested—for armed robbery and assault—and was in prison in Texas.

These are extreme examples. Most young people are not catapulted into a life of crime by the unfortunate circumstances of their youth. However, these examples show what profound and long-lasting effects a parental crisis can have on a vulnerable youngster. A broken home, a traumatic move, a parent incapacitated by illness may be one blow too many on a personality made fragile by the constant battering of misfortune.

All parents face crises during their children's formative years, and we can only do our best to maintain family stability during those times. Sometimes our best isn't good enough to prevent our children from being hurt, especially if the crisis occurs while they are approaching or into the particularly vulnerable stage of adolescence.

Psychologists agree that children need consistency and security. Many of us look back upon childhoods lacking in one or both elements. In turn—sometimes as a consequence—we were unable to provide a secure and consistent environment for our own children. Parents divorce, lose jobs, get sick, and sometimes die. They are susceptible to fear, anxiety, depression, and addiction. The consequences of a parental crisis can have a devastating effect on one child, a character-strengthening effect on another, depending upon the unique personality of each and the surrounding circumstances.

The way a child reacts during these life crises will have a profound effect on his or her future parent-child relationship. Parent/adult-child relationships are rooted in the early years. In adolescence the die is cast for the future.

QUESTIONS FOR YOU

1. How did the relationship between you and your child change during the child's adolescence?

2. In what ways did your adolescent rebel or pull away from parental authority?

3. How did you deal with it?

4. How have any "seeds of dissension" sown during your son's or daughter's adolescence sprouted into "wheat and tares" that affect your current relationship?

5. Were there circumstances in your family life—divorce, illness, financial crisis—that might have affected your parenting during those years?

6. If so, in what ways (if any) do you see yourself trying to make up for it now?

· 3 ·

Standing Watch
When Children Leave Home

Jarred awake by the shrill ring of the telephone, I lay staring into the shadowy corners of our bedroom. The luminous dial of the bedroom clock said 1:24 A.M. Apprehension tightened my throat and stiffened every muscle.

"Please, God." I breathed a prayer as Harry groped for the phone.

The big house was quiet. No creaking footsteps or rustle of blankets from the empty bedrooms above our heads. No flicker of headlights or crunch of gravel announcing someone's safe arrival home after a Saturday night date. A succession of graduations and weddings had left us with an empty nest. Yet I still cringed at the sound of sirens echoing through our valley, tires screeching at an intersection—or the telephone bell breaking the peaceful stillness of the night. Our fledglings had left the nest but not our hearts and minds.

"Wrong number," Harry grumbled, banging the receiver into its cradle. He'd had his own visions of disaster.

My sense of foreboding lifted but I lay awake, taking mental inventory of our scattered family. Somewhere within our far-flung circle, that very hour, one of our own might be in need of intercessory prayer.

- A daughter, alone too often while her young husband was on duty at the fire station—was she overwhelmed by the constant demands of a new baby?
- Another daughter, working at an all-night restaurant near the Southern California university where our son-in-law studied for his master's degree—was she exhausted after waiting tables until three in the morning?
- A son, married too early, trying to cope with the obligations of being a husband and expectant father—did he lie sleepless, too, wondering how he'd replace the job he'd lost?
- Another son, bypassing marriage to live with his girlfriend, trying to stay in school by working nights alone in a northern California service station—was he in danger and afraid?
- A daughter in her first year of college, dating another young man with shifty eyes and a doubtful reputation—was she drifting away from her Christian principles?
- A son, "bumming" around the streets of Santa Barbara, bent on joining the flower children of the decade and discarding the "materialistic" values of his parents' generation—would he get lost in the drug-infested subculture?

Our sons and daughters strained at the ties that bound them to us—ties that threatened to keep them from growing into independent, mature adults. They strained, and we felt the tug. Like young soldiers primed for battle, they were eager to prove themselves on the front lines of the world. But some of our children had gone off without their armor.

Ephesians 6:13 tells us to put on God's armor as protection against the evils of the world. But the verse continues: "And after you have done everything, to stand." God spoke to me—a mother—in those words. "After you have done everything, to stand."

We had done our best to arm our children for the challenges they would face beyond the security of hearth and home. But were they really ready? Were eighteen years—or nineteen or twentysome—of basic training enough to prepare our young recruits for the battles ahead?

And what does it mean, exactly, *to stand?* Stand back? Stand by? Or stand watch, as a sentry in enemy territory, ready to challenge intruders and sound alarms? Am I "standing" as I lay awake feeling the tug of our young adults pulling away from their childhood bonds?

Having Done Everything

Our mission as parents is to produce young people capable of assuming adult responsibilities. In pursuit of this goal, we allowed our children to take more and more responsibility for themselves as they matured. We saw them struggle and often fail as adolescents; we watch them struggle and often fail as they leave the cover of parental authority and protection. If we can watch them turn from dependence on us to reliance on their Father in heaven, we will have fulfilled our highest purpose as parents. "Then they would put their trust in God and would not forget his deeds but would keep his commands" (Ps. 78:7).

When basic training is over, as children reach the end of adolescence, we parents will see how well we have armed them for their coming battles. It's time for us to find our place behind the lines. We need to find the delicate balance— standing *back*, standing *by*, and standing *watch*—as our youngsters make their first tentative sorties into the adult world. We will sometimes be confused by mixed signals and will do one thing when we should be doing another!

Gwen and Hal were mortified when their daughter Sara, barely seventeen and a junior in high school, confessed she was pregnant. To make matters worse, the father was a young soldier just passing through town. Sara had dated him on the rebound after a stormy breakup with her steady boyfriend, Chuck. Sara and Chuck had gone together forever and everyone, including their parents, assumed they would be married after graduation from high school.

The greatest shock to Sara's family was that the baby's father was a relative stranger. Their Christian beliefs couldn't accommodate the idea of abortion. That left Sara and her parents to choose between two hard options: putting the baby up for adoption or keeping her. More questions surfaced: Could Sara as a single mother raise a child, or was there a possibility of a successful marriage to the young soldier? They talked far into the night.

"He *wants* to marry me," Sara insisted, her chin held high to still its quivering. "He's leaving for the West Coast next week, and I'll go with him."

Gwen burst into tears at the thought of her little girl giving birth to their first grandchild thousands of miles from home. "No, Sara, married or not, you'll have this baby right here where we can help you."

Gwen's tears triggered Hal's Irish temper. "She didn't need our help to get herself in this condition!" he roared, pounding the kitchen table where they'd been sitting since dinner. "And you, Gwen, have enough to do raising our own children. Sara made her bed. She'd better get used to lying in it!" He jerked open the refrigerator door for another beer.

As the oldest of five children, Sara felt she'd spent her life "fixing" things for them when they'd messed up. But no one could fix this for her. "I'm getting married and going out West," she said, pushing away from the table. She ran upstairs before her dad started shouting again.

TO STAND

I'll let Sara, whose daughter is now seventeen, relate the rest of her own story. "My poor parents didn't know what to do. Now that *I* have a seventeen-year-old, I understand what they must have been going through. Mother cried and Daddy yelled (and drank) and I withdrew into a shell until finally everyone decided that I'd marry my soldier, stay home until the baby was born, and then join him on the West Coast. In the meantime I could get enough units for my high school diploma by taking classes at night. I was bound and determined not to be a burden on my family.

"Daddy bellowed, but in the end he paid for my wedding and walked me down the aisle. He didn't do much to help my guilt, but he could have thrown me out, after all. I had a girlfriend whose family sent her packing when she came home pregnant. Although Daddy blew his top and Mother fell apart, I always knew they cared about me.

"I have never felt so alone or afraid in my whole life as the Sunday afternoon they put six-week-old Tiffany and me on the plane for California. I'd seen Chuck, my true love from high school, at church that morning and he had looked miserable. I'd wanted to fall into his arms and tell him how sorry I was, but I'd just looked the other way. I was married to someone else—someone I hardly knew. I hung on to my baby girl and prayed for God to take care of us.

"I look back over the years and see how God *has* taken care of us, in spite of all the mistakes both my parents and I made. I learned new lessons at every fork in the road. My first marriage was definitely not made in heaven. It began on a sour note and went steadily downhill from there. After a few miserable months I left the California desert and went home to the lakes and trees of the Midwest. Mother and Daddy met me at the plane and asked me what my plans were for the future.

"In the back of my mind I'd hoped, or maybe expected, they'd want me to come home again, but I was too proud to let on. After all, I was eighteen—old enough to be on my own. I asked my parents if Tiffany and I could stay with them for a few days until I found a job and a place to live. We slept on the sofa in the den, because my sister had taken over my old room. She loved Tiff, though, so I hired her to baby-sit after school while I clerked in the local grocery store. Nights I did free-lance typing in the studio apartment we rented.

"In between working and taking care of my baby, I had no energy or opportunity for any social life. I didn't even go around my family much, because I wanted to prove how independent I could be. My friends from school were all having the time of their lives, and I guess I felt pretty sorry for myself. Apparently Mother and Daddy felt sorry for me, too, because they eventually invited me to come home. Mother and Sis took care of Tiff so I could work longer days and give up my night job. Chuck came back into my life. God allowed us to fall in love all over again, in a more mature way, and we were married. I'd thought when I got pregnant with Tiffany that no one could fix the mess I'd made of my life, but the Lord could and did.

"Looking back I understand how much courage and love it took for my parents to choose to let me go. Imagine putting a teenager and a tiny baby on a plane, sending them off to a distant state and a son-in-law they hardly knew! I don't know if I could do that with Tiffany, or even if it would be right.

"My family was what they call dysfunctional, and I was better off out of there for a while. My dad had a drinking problem that kept us in a state of turmoil. It was the 'elephant in the living room' that everyone very carefully tiptoed around. No one talked about it. Instead, we poured all our emotional energies into fixing the damage caused by Dad's drunken episodes.

"My pregnancy topped every crisis we'd ever had! When I got on that plane for California, I was sure that I'd torn our family apart for good. I saw myself as a 'bad girl' for getting pregnant and believed I had some basic character weakness that kept me from doing what I was supposed to do as the eldest daughter—keep peace in my family.

"My months in California, as awful as they were, helped me to grow up and disconnect emotionally from my family.

Although I was disappointed not to be welcomed home immediately when I returned to the Midwest, my months in our little apartment underscored my emotional separation. Then, when Tiff and I went back home to live, my focus was on taking charge of my life. I concentrated on my job, my baby, and my social life. I wasn't so dependent on the emotional climate of the family. I was usually rushing off somewhere.

"It must have been hard for my parents to accept the crumbs of relationship I offered them. They stood by me as I made my mistakes and struggled to recover from them. It must have been incredibly hard for them to allow me to move in again with them, working and dating at my convenience, while they helped baby-sit Tiffany and helped us financially. They weren't getting much back from me. They watched me finish growing up according to *my* standards, not theirs. I appreciate that they never once said, 'See, we told you so. We knew you couldn't do this alone. Now we're ready to help you on our terms!' They neither said those words nor implied them, and I admire their restraint.

"The irony, in human terms, is that God took our broken family in crisis and allowed a pregnancy that could have been devastating to be the very thing that pushed us all on to an extremely difficult journey toward health."

Gwen and Hal are good examples of parents who choose to "stand" in a variety of ways while their sons and daughters make mistakes and learn to live with the consequences.

Standing By. With all their weaknesses and conflicts, Hal and Gwen were there when Sara needed to know that someone cared, standing by as she wrestled with her decision to marry her young soldier and keep her baby. They were willing to involve themselves in the situation and consider the options for a solution to the problem of her pregnancy. They were available but did not make demands.

Sara says, "I've never had a moment's doubt that Tiffany belonged with me, and I'm grateful that my family didn't press for the alternative of putting her up for adoption."

Standing by is being available. It's loving and caring, expressing concern, and lending moral support, even when we don't approve of the choices our young adults are making. Standing by is allowing emerging adults to take charge of their own lives, ready or not. It's allowing them to pull away from our authority and control to develop a firm sense of *selfhood*. Standing by is not saying "I told you so," when the choices our maturing children make lead them into deeper waters. It's being willing to back off or reach out at the appropriate time.

Standing Back, Letting Go. Sara's parents stood by, letting her know they cared; though hurt and angry, they were willing to listen and talk, and, finally, willing to stand back while she pulled away and went to California.

Sara says, "Mother told me just recently that she felt I'd abandoned her when I left for the West Coast. I wondered how she could have expected me to be thinking of *her* needs when I was so taken up with my own! We were both fighting for survival. I can see I needed to leave. I couldn't handle the challenge of motherhood and continue to play Miss Fix-It in my family at the same time.

"My parents really backed off for the months I was in California, which is surprising considering my mother's feelings of abandonment. Maybe she was being a silent martyr, but I think she was really trying to give me space and find new ways of coping with the situation at home. When she called me, she never dumped her problems on me or hinted that I should come home, even though she knew me well enough to read the misery between the lines of my letters. I would never have come out and admitted that I'd made a mistake. Ah, the pride of youth."

Standing Guard. When Sara returned to her hometown, her parents continued to stand back for a while. Wounds still needed time to heal. Hal was still disappointed and angry.

Gwen still stung with feelings of rejection at Sara's "abandonment" of her when she opted to go to California. If Sara wanted to go it alone, so be it, Gwen thought. Although Gwen ached to involve herself in Sara's life as the traditional doting grandma, her daughter's independent attitude held her back. Sara had changed in the months she'd been away.

Sara *didn't* want to go it alone, but her pride kept her from crying out for the help and support she really needed. She was determined to show her parents that she could get by, especially when she remembered what her dad had said about learning to lie in the bed she had made. One night she came home from work to find Tiffany sick with a high fever. Sis, who had been caring for her little niece, insisted that they call Gwen, who came within moments. By this time, Sara's parents had shifted into the role of standing guard—watching to see how Sara was managing and getting progress reports from Sis, their younger daughter. Gwen had been waiting for a call and came to Sara's side, feeling maternal concern and a sense of triumph that maybe the cold war was dissolving. Love was the victor, transcending the tension in the relationship.

"I saw a new strength in my mother that night when she took Tiffany out of my arms, ordered me to run cool water into the tub, and sent Sis to the store for rubbing alcohol. At home with my dad she always seemed so indecisive, but she knew exactly what needed to be done for a sick baby.

"After that my dad started dropping in or stopping at my check stand in the grocery store to ask how we were doing. Within a few weeks he came to me with the invitation to move home. He said they'd been watching us and saw how hard it was for me to work two jobs and take care of Tiffany and he thought they could help if I'd let them. Would I let them! It didn't take me long to pack our things. Sis doubled up again with my little sister, and Tiffany and I moved into my old room.

"Our family hadn't suddenly gone from dysfunctional to

healthy, but the patterns of interaction between family members had changed. In my absence, the younger kids had learned to depend more on themselves and one another. If they tried to put me back in my old fix-it role, I was usually too involved with my own concerns to be helpful. With Tiffany underfoot, Mother was too busy playing grandma to think about how many beers Daddy had had that week. Since her attention wasn't riveted on every move he made, there was less friction between them. That seemed to change the atmosphere of the whole household. The alcoholism and the codependency were still there, but I had gotten out of the center of it."

The course of events in Sara's life had gradually changed the patterns of interaction in her family network. Her parents first *stood by* while she made crucial decisions for her immediate future, then *stood back* while she played out her decisions to marry and leave the state. When she returned to the Midwest, they responded to the changed circumstances by *standing guard*, watching from a distance while Sara tested her independence on friendly soil. They stood like sentries between their daughter and whatever might threaten her safety as she took on adult responsibility.

Although Sara moved home again for a time, restoring her parents' stand-by position, the relationship between Gwen and Hal and their daughter had changed in a positive way.

A CIRCUITOUS ROUTE

Like many of her generation, Sara's first break from home was not her last. It is not unusual for the emerging adult to test the waters several times before taking the final plunge into independence.

Have you seen the Family Circus cartoons where Billy is sent on a brief errand and arrives at his destination only after a complicated and roundabout trail through the neighborhood? He is delayed and diverted by the attractions along his meandering way, always within shouting range of home base as he explores every possibility for adventure.

Young people are like that. They very often take a circuitous route between adolescence and adulthood and create an emotional roller-coaster ride for their parents in the process!

Jill, the mother of two young adults, said, "Dawn was so uncharacteristically crabby for a couple of months before she left for college that I was almost glad to see her go. On the other hand, every time anyone would ask me about her, I'd feel like crying. I'd thoroughly enjoyed the fun and excitement of her teenage years, and I wasn't ready to let go of that stage of life.

"Dawn apparently wasn't ready, either, and was probably just acting out her own insecurities by being edgy and temperamental. She'd chosen to go to college because that's what her friends were doing. It was the wrong decision for her. Within a few weeks she was on the phone—in tears—asking if she could come home again, and of course we said yes. She was a little embarrassed, but she pulled herself together and found a challenging job in our community. The career-girl image seemed to fit Dawn more comfortably than the collegiate one she'd tried, and she was soon back to her old cheerful self.

"We were just getting used to the new routine in our household when she decided to move out again and share an apartment with a couple of girlfriends. I was about to turn her bedroom into a home office when one of the girls left the apartment to get married and the other two couldn't make the rent. Dawn came home again.

"While all this was going on, we were dealing with Jordan, Dawn's younger brother, who was the classic adolescent rebel. From the time he hit sixteen and got his driver's license, it was a constant battle, especially between Jordan and his dad. They had just about come to blows the week

Dawn moved home for the second time, and I was a wreck. Jordan was packing to leave "forever" as Dawn was unpacking to stay for who knew how long. I can smile now, because I think both kids have gotten beyond the yo-yo stage, but it was a painful time."

All kinds of traumatic events may lead up to and accompany young adults' separation from their childhood homes. They are torn between the familiarity of childhood and the mysteries of adulthood, between the safety and security of family and friends and the loneliness of living among strangers in a strange land, between irresponsibility and being held accountable. *Torn* is a proper adjective for this condition, for there is a tearing of ties. We don't make "clean" breaks with our families.

When the door finally closes (or slams) behind our emerging adult, we are licking our own wounds—for there has been tearing on both ends of the ties that bind. We are sad or relieved or frightened or resigned at the wrenching separation from the flesh of our flesh. When the amputation is finally accomplished it is sometimes hard to hear, "Mom, can I come home again?" But it is vital that we not lock the door behind them too quickly, before they turn the corner or leave the neighorhood. It is important to refrain from collapsing beds and stowing away childhood treasures, just in case.

They may be reluctant to admit it, but our young adults like to think of their bedrooms, like their parents, as freeze-framed in their old places, always available in case of emergency.

Doctors Jeffrey and Carol Rubin write:

> It is important for our children to know that their decisions in early adulthood are not unalterable. Although we would not want to encourage their making decisions foolishly, knowing that they can always go home again, it is important for them to know that going home is a possibility, that there is still that place that one

can return after sorties out into the world to test possibilities and wings.[1]

S.O.S. CALLS

Emergencies will happen, whether or not they are drastic enough to send the newly independent child home again.

There are the financial kind, as in "I *had* to take advantage of that great sale on CDs" (That's compact discs, not certificates of deposit). "The landlord made us pay for the broken shower door, even though it was cracked when we moved in." "Would you believe that outfit that sent me the credit card charges *eighteen percent* interest on the unpaid balance!"

There are medical emergencies: "I stepped on a nail at work and the doctor wants to give me a tetanus shot. Is that what I'm allergic to, or was it tetracycline?" "Marci cut her hand while she was helping me wallpaper the kitchen, and we think it needs stitches. Could my insurance pay for that even though we're not married? I *am* still covered under your policy, aren't I?" "Mama, I've been so sick with the flu. I wish I had the strength to get up and fix myself some of that chicken soup you used to make."

And there will be emotional crises: "I'm not staying in this town one more minute. I couldn't bear to run into Peter after what happened between us." "I guess you and Dad were right about this marriage. It's not working out."

SELF-DEFENSE

Between phone calls and distress signals we parents are in the process of reorganizing our own lives. "Being there" for our kids is easier if we know where *we* are. While you're giving your children space to work out their strategies for survival, take inventory of your own resources and work on strengthening your own defense system. A friend reminds me that the best thing I can offer my grown children is my whole, healthy self.

Harry and I congratulated ourselves (with equal measures of pride and gratitude) on being *available* when our teenagers and young adults needed us. We were recovering alcoholics when we married, so being available—literally and emotionally—was an important step for us. Although our resources were limited in the beginning years of recovery, a gracious God encouraged us by showing us the progress we'd made. The healthier we became, the more we had to give to our children as they left home.

Give Up the Lead

There comes a time when a parent is forced to loosen the grip and concede victory in the war for independence. The former days of being a benevolent dictator—directing and protecting, demanding and comforting, omnipotent in a child's eyes—come to an end. Eventually we loosen and untie the proverbial apron strings or they will be torn from our grasp.

Our children will acquire their share of psychological bumps and bruises as they fumble their way toward maturity. We can no more prevent that than we could prevent the skinned knees they acquired as toddlers learning to walk and run. We will continue to feel their pain each time they stumble and fall; it's a fact of parenthood.

So often the pain seems unnecessary. If only they could benefit from our experience, we think. We're old veterans of life's battle; we know where the booby traps are. If only they'd let us, we'd willingly share our strategies for victory. By trial and error, we've developed a design for living that's worked for us. We've done the ground work, and it's hard to understand why our children insist on risking everything by blazing new trails through the jungle this side of adulthood. All they'd need to do is follow in our tracks and get on with life. Right? Wrong. Our children are not extensions of ourselves. They are unique personalities with their own ways of looking at things. Much as we would like them to accept our chosen lifestyle with its values and taboos, their need is to sift and sort whatever we've given them on their way to independence. They will discard things we have treasured, and they will take with them things fit for burning.

We cannot go with our children into adulthood; they will have to conquer their own ground, as we did. But we can keep the home fires burning and the welcome mat out, sensitive to the signals we receive from their battleground and ready for a time when our young adult needs a temporary "R and R" or a chance to fall back and regroup. "Having done everything," we can only cover them in the armor of our prayers as they go forward.

- We can stand by, alert and available, as our young adults test their independence.
- We can stand back, mouths shut and hands off, as they learn from sometimes painful experience.
- We can stand guard, ready to bring veteran strength to the battle, in case real danger threatens to defeat them.

QUESTIONS FOR YOU

1. What concerns did you have about your young adults when they first left home?

2. Did you feel that you'd done enough to prepare them for independent living?

3. Did you experience the "yo-yo syndrome" of many families, as young adults move in and out again before the final separation? How did you feel about that?

4. In what ways have you stood by, stood back, or stood guard while your children made the transition to independence?

5. If you had been Sara's parents, how would you have handled her untimely pregnancy?

6. Have you ever felt abandoned, as Gwen did, when one of your adult children left home?

7. Did the absence of your young adult create changes in your home atmosphere or patterns of interaction between other members of the family? In a positive or negative way?

8. Did your relationship with your adult child change during the separation process?

• 4 •

Cease-Fire
The Generation Gap Narrows

Most of our interfamily relationships ebb and flow somewhere between the extremes of intimacy and estrangement. We are inclined to go from periods of harmony with our adult children to times of clashing discord, from waging war to waving white flags of peace. Where we clutch at the familiar security of our parental authority roles, our maturing children fight to escape our bondage and move ahead into new territory. Where our children, in later years, are content with our rear-guard positions, we rebel at the restrictions of our retirement and press for closer involvement with their world. We vie for position, conquer (or surrender) the next hill, and finally settle onto another peaceful plateau.

Periods of peace mark the progress of the ever-evolving parent/adult-child relationship. A cease-fire is a truce. The peaceful plateau we find ourselves on may be only a temporary respite from further conflict between generations. Land mines wait beneath the tranquil surface to explode and disrupt the tenuous peace. We can either tiptoe away from renewed conflict or step toward enduring peace as we seek to narrow the generation gap.

LOWERING OUR DEFENSES

The post-adolescent period can be a time when both parents and children begin to lower their defenses and move toward restoring trust and closeness. When our emerging adults finally break free of our authority and move out on their own, showing us and themselves that they can cope with their adult roles, a new kind of peace reigns.

In our family, this was a particularly pleasant time of interaction with our grown children. Since there was only a seven-year span between the oldest and the youngest of our combined brood, we went fairly quickly from the intensity of a house exploding with teenagers to the proverbial empty nest.

In actuality, Harry and I were rarely alone for long in our empty nest. Our young adults came and went, home on a school holiday or for an hour to wash a load of clothes. On Sundays I made spaghetti or inside-out ravioli for whoever might be hungry for a family dinner—or hungry, period. The young marrieds had a standing invitation and before long were lugging high chairs and diaper bags to our minireunions. During the week someone might stop in to borrow a paintbrush or a pan for the new apartment or just to share a bit of news over a cup of coffee. I loved every minute of it. Our emancipated young adults were coming "home" voluntarily instead of looking for excuses to escape our constant surveillance.

It was no wonder that our newly adult children enjoyed our company more than they had during their chaotic teenage years. We no longer greeted them at the door with, "Where have you been? Who were you with? Do you know what time it is?" Instead it was, "Hi! Come in! How about a sandwich? We were hoping you'd stop by!" All of us felt new freedom in the release from our old assignments of authority and submission. We began to be more like peers, sharing grown-up concerns, gradually discovering a new basis for relationship. Stimulated by new interests and changing lifestyles, we were eager to share our lives with one another.

Our children had come to adulthood acting like they knew it all but secretly afraid that they didn't, afraid that maybe they couldn't make it out there in the world. Now they were discovering their own capabilities and feeling good about themselves. With an increase in their self-confidence, they were less defensive.

What had happened? We'd backed off and yielded some of our adult territory, welcoming our children into our formerly exclusive "adult" ranks, seeing them as individuals with identities separate from ourselves. In return, as we demonstrated our willingness to let them lead their own lives, they'd cautiously torn down the protective walls they'd built around themselves. While walking toward independence, they'd wanted no interference from clinging parents. With dependency ties severed, they'd let us into formerly forbidden areas, where they paraded their independence before us. We had swallowed our criticism and applauded them and ourselves for surviving the civil-war years of adolescence. We were friendly allies at last.

TIGHTENING THE BONDS

As two of our daughters celebrated their twentieth wedding anniversaries this year, I felt a twinge of nostalgia, remembering the special closeness between us in those exciting days of their early womanhood. Twenty years ago, as we chose flowers for the ceremonies, addressed invitations, and tied scoopfuls of rice into little net bags, new woman-to-woman relationships were born.

Although I knew their coming vows would separate us in some ways and that our sons-in-law would outrank me as an intimate forever, I felt secure in my place as mother of the brides. With vicarious delight, I dug through the cherry hutch for Grandma's crocheted tablecloth and crytal goblets, heirlooms I'd received from my mother, "something old" to grace the tables of new homes where I could only be a guest.

As the babies arrived, I took on the grandmother role with relish, forging new bonds and strengthening old ones. My daughters and I were connected like links in a generational chain. Judith Viorst writes about this phenomenon from the perspective of the adult child:

> Parenthood—our parenthood—can serve a reconciling function by giving our parents better parts to play, by freeing them to be—as grandma and grandpa—more loving, indulgent, tender, patient, generous, you name it, than they had ever been as mother and father. No longer concerned with instilling moral values, no longer in charge of discipline and rules, no longer dedicated to building character, they become their best selves, and we—in our pleasure at all they can offer our children—begin to forgive them their sins, both real and imagined.[1]

As a grandmother, I had a "better part to play" than I could have imagined.

Those were precious but fleeting days of mother-daughter love reinforced. We had come through the adolescent rebellion to the camaraderie of women sharing in the secret wonder of nest building. I, the mother, knew the way and—for a while—was the accepted leader of our sisterhood. My daughters were not biological sisters but loving friends, whose close bond had developed within the context of our blended family. As young women they shared their special friendship with me and welcomed my involvement in their lives. Who else, after all, would stay up half the night sewing rosepoint lace onto cotton brocade for the spring wedding or struggling with yards of purple velvet for winter bridesmaids? Who else would shed such compassionate tears over labor pains begun too early or understand so deeply the joy of a preemie's victorious hold on life?

I cherish the memories of those days, but they were as transitory as the honeymoons. Changes in our circumstances demanded that we move onto new ground and find a new basis for our relationships.

ERECTING BARRIERS TO PEACE

Not all families experience a post-adolescent cease-fire. Where rifts between parents and adult children continue beyond the adolescent rebellion, pride is usually to blame. Pride: a child's defense against criticism; a parent's shield against rejection.

At nineteen or twenty, young people are expected to take their places in the adult world. For this awesome task they need all the confidence they can muster, but we parents are apt to fail them by diminishing what little they have. (Remember that arrogance is usually a big cover-up.) When we disapprove of a grown child's choice of career, political philosophy, or love partner we are resorting to old habits of parenting. We barge in with unsolicited advice instead of trusting acceptance. When we dismiss or ridicule our children's ideas and goals, we undermine their self-esteem. They respond defensively.

Kirk tells of his struggle to make peace with his father. "I suppose it was my pride," he says, "but I still think my old man was wrong to cut me off like he did. He had his mind set on me going to his college, so I went ahead and sent in my application and all, even though I wasn't sure in my own mind what I wanted to do. Then, right when we found out I'd been accepted, I got this great opportunity to go into the music business with some guys I knew. Dad and I butted heads over that for a couple of weeks, with me trying to find a reasonable compromise and him slinging insults about my 'weird' taste in music and my choice of friends. I wanted to give it a few months trial and then, if we couldn't make it as a rock group, go to college the following year.

"The upshot was that I could either go to school on his time schedule or I was on my own, right now, period, end of support. I thought he was being grossly unfair. My friends' parents thought the idea of our forming a band was cool and didn't lay down any ultimatums about 'do it my way or else.' I moved in with one of them for a while. Our group was pretty good, and we got a few gigs—even cut a record—but there's a lot of competition out there, and we eventually fell apart. It took about four years after that for my dad and me to start speaking again, and things are okay between us now. I'll never be sorry I tried it, though. And he'll never understand. Dad thinks I've grown up and come to my senses, but I really came back for the sake of Mom and the rest of the family. I had to swallow my pride a little, but family is family."

Kirk's father, Jack, doesn't see himself as responsible for the tension that is still evident between the two men. Kirk's sister says you can sometimes "cut the tension with a knife" at family gatherings. Their truce is one of convenience, and their peace, fragile.

SETTLING FOR A TEMPORARY TRUCE

Like Kirk and his father, many of us get stuck in our relationships midway between total estrangement and the mutual affection and loving alliance that close family members can enjoy. We settle for a surface politeness while our hearts mourn the loss of an intimacy we once knew.

Jack remembers the days of father-son hikes in the nearby foothills, teaching Kirk to fish the streams and find the hidden trails and, at day's end, to coax a lively blaze from a handful of damp twigs. He remembers the admiration of an eleven-year-old for a father who seemed to know everything and how it made him feel stronger and braver than the bronze stars he'd earned during the Korean conflict. That admiration had gotten lost somewhere during the years that followed, when Kirk had pulled away into some adolescent world where Jack couldn't follow.

"Kirk wasn't anything like I was as a teenager," Jack said. "I kept on working with Pop on the farm and I showed him some respect, too. Sure, the old man wasn't always so smart about everything. Sometimes, I'm ashamed to say, I'd deliberately show him up by using a little high school math that he'd either forgotten or never known. Even so, I looked up to him. I wouldn't have thought of disappointing him by abandoning my education for some harebrained scheme like starting a rock group!"

Jack had been sure it wouldn't work, but his advice had fallen on deaf ears. Wasn't Kirk paying the price for his stubbornness now—trying to get somewhere in the business world without a college education?

Jack doesn't recognize his own stubbornness as an issue to be dealt with. "We've patched things up a little, but neither of us is going to open an old can of worms by bringing up the whole issue again. We can be civil enough to each other and that's okay for now. I'd as soon let sleeping dogs lie. Someday Kirk will see that I was right."

Both Kirk and his father yearn for understanding, but each waits for the other to concede his error, and neither wants to risk losing the peaceful ground they've gained, however tenuous. They look back on the years of estrangement and remember the hurt. So they carefully sidestep any subject that might stir up old conflict, keeping the peace, such as it is. Jack has accepted a sleeping-dog atmosphere; Kirk says, "Things are okay."

Many of us fail to reconnect with our adult children after the revolutionary skirmishes of adolescence. There have been casualties on both sides. We erect barriers of pride against further hurt and settle for an uneasy truce.

CONFRONTING THE ENEMY

Pride, the enemy of peace, is the chief weakness of fallible humankind. I have talked to dozens of people whose families are, or have been, torn apart by dissension. In *every* case, pride was the hammer that drove the wedge between individuals. Where whole families were drawn into battle, pride spearheaded the attack.

Hurt pride has hardened my friend Marie's words: "I'd like a closer relationship with Joanne, but she keeps me at a distance, and that's the way she seems to want it. I really don't think she cares how her dad and I feel, anyway, because she's always ignored any suggestions or advice we had to offer and done her own thing. We're not happy with the situation as it is, but we have our own lives. It doesn't matter anymore. I sure don't care enough to start a row about it."

I look at the skirmishes and cold wars in my own life— and keep coming back to pride. A few years ago my own hurt pride was responsible for cooling the formerly warm and loving relationship I'd had with my youngest daughter, Nancy. She gave me permission to write about our experience. Nancy was a senior in college when I sensed that she was pulling away from some of the Christian principles she'd upheld since her conversion in high school. When I criticized her lifestyle and warned her of problems she might be facing, she brushed me off. My criticism and her independence widened the gap between us.

I was recovering from surgery for breast cancer when Nancy applied for a master's program in a midwestern seminary. I knew she was taking that opportunity to escape a dead-end romance, and I was relieved to see her returning to her faith, but I was secretly hurt that she would go so far away when I was in precarious health. My pride kept me from expressing my feelings to her (and trying to understand her position), and my hurt turned to a gnawing resentment that continued to eat at our mother-daughter bond. Years later, with the birth of her first baby, she reached out to me in her need and a true healing of our relationship followed. We reconciled as two adult women and our bond is stronger than ever.

After I wrote the previous paragraphs, it seemed only fair to offer Nancy equal time to tell her side of the story. These are her words:

"During the summer before my senior year in college, I fell into a relationship which proved to be quite abusive and a very negative experience for me. I remember my mom's criticism of the relationship from its onset. I was confused and defensive. As the relationship progressed, my self-esteem and confidence in my own judgment plummeted. I poured myself into school while denying that there was anything unhealthy about my relationship. I do not remember helpful suggestions coming from my mother. But chances are I would have turned a deaf ear if they had.

"By the end of the year I had figured a way out of the relationship and a few months later a way out of my life as I had known it. I was ready to start over with a new goal and a new life in a new state. I was aware of my mom's illness, but I believed she would be fine with the proper medical care. Besides, my own life was too overwhelming to really allow her problems to impact me.

"I believe that much of the tension between my mom and me was due to my awareness of her disappointment in me and my lifestyle. Once I made a concerted effort to change, to live out my faith, I felt like she thought I was a hypocrite. In reality I was projecting my negative thoughts of guilt and shame onto my mother, so that when we encountered one another our relationship was filled with much tension.

"It was not until I had my first baby and was in a helpless situation that I began to let down my guard. We still had our tense moments, but they gradually subsided."

When we are hurt and disappointed by those closest to us, we whip out our shields of pride and cringe behind them—or draw swords and jab at our adversaries in retaliation.

The book of Proverbs warns us about pride. "Pride only

breeds quarrels, but wisdom is found in those who take advice" (Prov. 13:10).

Seminars, support groups, and professional counselors are available at every turn for our edification. Libraries overflow with how-to books. Secular or spiritual, truth is truth wherever we find it. Advice is cheap, plentiful, and often wise, but how shall we apply it when pride keeps getting in the way?

Christians seeking advice can and should turn to the Word of God. "Sharper than any double-edged sword, it penetrates even to dividing soul and spirit, joints and marrow; it judges the thoughts and attitudes of the heart" (Heb. 4:12). Can we expose ourselves to such a fearsome promise and let God's Word cut through our shields of pride? We can if we are serious about seeking and maintaining real peace with our adult children. If we can see ourselves in God's light, we will be humble. If we really know ourselves, we cannot be proud.

Pat and Lloyd allowed God's word to speak to them as they sought reconciliation with their son and daughter-in-law.

"I'm ashamed to confess that our reliance on Scripture was a last-ditch effort at making peace with Keith and his family," Pat said. "Not that we hadn't prayed diligently and asked the Lord's intervention, but we hadn't thought to look in the Bible for specific answers to our dilemma. God finally got through to us during a Sunday-morning sermon. I'll start at the beginning and tell you what happened.

"Keith's older brother, Aaron, came to us for a loan to help him start a new business. Lloyd and I talked about it and decided to put up the money. It was a good investment in Aaron's future and a good business investment for us. We should have known that Keith would get wind of it and resent it. He's always been jealous of Aaron and thought we were partial to him, although that just isn't true. The problem was we'd had to turn Keith down a couple of years before when he'd wanted money. At that time, our ready cash had been tied up in CDs, and we hadn't been particularly enthusiastic about Keith's plans for spending the money he thought he needed. We'd practically forgotten about that incident when we granted Aaron the loan.

"When Keith and his family began giving us the cold shoulder, we were bewildered—until we heard from other members of our family that it was all about our loan to Aaron. Keith resented our giving money to Aaron when we'd refused him. At first we couldn't believe that he would react that way; then we felt terrible to think he'd been carrying a grudge for so long. The strain and friction between us seemed out of proportion to the cause, and we waited for it to blow over as other family misunderstandings had. But it went on and on. We kept making tentative overtures to Keith and his wife, Eva, and getting nowhere. Even the grandchildren were cold as ice toward us.

"After a while Lloyd and I began to get angry with them for treating us so shabbily, when we hadn't intended to hurt anyone. We rehashed all of our reasons for our past decisions about both our sons, and it all seemed perfectly reasonable to us. We felt we were the innocent victims in the whole mess. One Sunday, after we hadn't seen or heard from anyone in Keith's family for a month, we heard a sermon that prodded us into action. It was based on Matthew 5:23–24:

> Therefore, if you are offering your gift at the altar and there remember that your brother has something against you, leave your gift there in front of the altar. First go and be reconciled to your brother; then come and offer your gift.

"I knew for sure that those verses of Scripture were for us. Keith and Eva were Christians—our brother and sister in Christ. We couldn't ignore God's directive to 'go and be reconciled.'

"We went, I admit, a little reluctantly, dragging our

resentment behind us. We'd gotten pretty disgruntled and defensive about the whole situation and didn't feel like we should have to make the first move toward peace, but we knew God had spoken to us. The whole family had gotten involved by that time. Keith wasn't speaking to Aaron, and Aaron was unhappy with his younger sister, Beth, who had made the mistake of telling Keith about Aaron's loan. Beth's husband, who was Aaron's good buddy, was angry with her for talking out of turn. Even the cousins were taking sides. It was a tangled web and we were caught in the middle.

"Lloyd and I prayed about it and decided to drive to Keith's house that very afternoon. He and Eva were out in the garage painting patio furniture. They barely acknowledged our presence, and I know it was only the grace of God that overruled our pride and kept us from turning around and going home in a huff. We pressed on until they were willing to sit down and talk.

"We told them that we'd felt hurt and misunderstood and that we wanted to explain our side of the issue. They listened, although at first they denied that the loan to Aaron had caused the problem. They did have some other grievances, and we gave them room to express them. It was obvious that all of us had been hurting. We wanted to forgive and forget and put it behind us.

"Although we didn't completely resolve every misunderstanding right then and there, that Sunday afternoon marked a turning point in our relationship. Before it was over we were all crying and hugging and saying how much we'd missed each other.

"In being honest about our feelings we had overcome the biggest block between us. If we didn't understand anything else about each other, we understood our love and need for each other. Our strained relationship had thrown our family out of balance and none of us liked it. There was—probably still is—some misunderstanding about the whole loan fiasco, but we're all willing and anxious to get beyond that incident."

The conflict that developed in Pat and Lloyd's family affected every member. After peace was restored between the adults, Aaron overheard his twelve-year-old daughter talking to her younger cousin. "I don't know what we were supposed to be mad about," she said, "but I'm glad we can go to the movies together again."

When hurt pride results in estrangement between parents and their adult children, both sides suffer loss. Our children may keep us at a distance, but they want our approval and acceptance just as we want their love and understanding. We may tell ourselves, like Marie, that we don't care, but we can't stop caring. It's that caring that will keep us seeking paths to an enduring peace.

KEEPING THE PEACE

Peace, according to the *Zondervan Pictorial Bible Dictionary*, is used "throughout the Bible to indicate a spirit of tranquility and freedom from either inward or outward disturbance. When nations enjoyed this, it was regarded as a gift from God."[2]

In a peaceful world, nations respect each other's boundaries, yet are open and hospitable to each other. They share resources. They support, aid, and comfort one another in times of natural calamity or threat by hostile nations. They learn each other's languages so that they can communicate more effectively.

Is that an achievable goal for human beings—for parents and adult children—as well as nations? Let's take those conditions one by one.

We respect one another's boundaries. Recently the entire world was in turmoil when Iraq invaded its neighbor Kuwait. The marauders overturned the government, raped and pillaged their way through the tiny country, and brought the surrounding nations to war.

On a smaller scale, one interfering parent can wreak havoc in the life of an adult child. Many a divorce has been laid at the feet of a despotic dad or a meddling mother-in-law. Many an ongoing family feud has been triggered by the invasion of a prying parent into an adult child's life. Sometimes our excuse is that we don't know where our child's boundaries lie and are confused by the changing terrain, but if we respect our adult children as equals, if we are sensitive to their signals, we can learn to read the road signs they put out for us. Respecting a child as an adult—an adult who is independent, like a country over which we have no authority—is a giant step toward parenthood, rather than parenting.

We are open and hospitable. World War Two left Germany divided into two nations. The notorious Berlin Wall dividing a city stood as a constant reminder of hostility between the two neighbors. As long as the wall stood, there was little chance of a unified Germany.

The revolution of adolescence shouldn't create a permanent division, and it won't if both generations resist the temptation to nurse their wounds behind walls of pride.

We share our resources. Although the United States is a country rich in natural resources, we import coffee from Brazil, diamonds from Africa, fine wool from Scotland—all products that add pleasure and beauty to our lives. We export valuable commodities around the world, sometimes sustaining life and health among the people of other countries.

Parents and their adult children have an abundance to give one another. At different stages of our relationships, one may be richer and another poorer, one stronger and another weaker. There's a "balance of trade" that must be handled with diplomacy.

As we of the older generation remain open to the ideas

and respectful of the opinions of our younger adults, they will be more receptive to the acquired wisdom of our experience.

We support, aid, and comfort one another. A terrifying earthquake in Mexico City, boatloads of starving Vietnamese refugees drifting on the high seas, or a devastating flood in Bangladesh brings rescue missions from compassionate countries throughout the world. One nation rushes to the aid of another when disaster strikes.

Our natural response to children in crisis is to run to their side—if they will permit it. Where we have established friendly relations with our children, where we have kept our borders free of pride shields and roadblocks, they will let us in to give the help we yearn to give.

We learn each other's languages. The United Nations defines 223 distinct nations, countries, and territories around the world. Leaders, ambassadors, and other diplomatic representatives of these countries are frequent guests at the White House. Many converse fluently in English, widening the field of understanding between people of different cultures and nationalities.

As our children matured, they moved beyond the mysterious language of adolescence, where they'd sabotaged our efforts to communicate by inventing new words and investing old ones with new meanings. *Cool* meant hot and *bad* meant good and every parental phrase was suspect. When they entered the adult world, they began to communicate in our language. Sometimes we are put off by a youthful accent and are tempted to fall into old habits of sermonizing, but we will risk losing communication unless we resist. On both sides, thoughtless words can kindle old flames of misunderstanding.

Our attempts at communication may sometimes create temporary discord, but these clashes can be the growing pains of a deepening relationship. The proverbial generation gap, perhaps at its narrowest during the cease-fire of the post-adolescent period, will widen and narrow again for the duration of our parent/adult-child relationships. With every widening gap we may need to build new bridges of communication.

The conditions outlined above can apply to maintaining good relationships between generations as well as between countries. We can use them as guidelines as we seek an enduring peace with our adult children.

CHANGING POSITIONS

A cease-fire is a truce, a suspension of hostilities between belligerents. A truce is a good place to start after any breach of relations, but it is not true peace. An enduring peace between parents and their adult children—as between countries—demands a constant shifting of positions and adjusting of roles to fit the changing pattern of our lives and the lives of our children.

Keeping the peace between generations requires work and willingness to change. We are repeatedly challenged to find new grounds for relationships with our adult children. If we are to move beyond our peaceful plateaus, we will need to be flexible, which is increasingly difficult as we become older and more set in our ways! We are apt to stubbornly stand our conquered ground and demand our territorial rights.

"But we've *always* had the whole family together on Christmas morning!"

"You can't be serious about moving to Alabama! When will we see our grandchildren?"

"You *used* to have time to stop by on Sunday afternoons. I guess your new friends are more important than family."

And there came a day when the grandbabies, who had once seemed to belong to me as much as to their parents, placed a subtle wedge between my daughters and me.

"Mom, we'd like to come to dinner on Sunday, but Craig has a cold and it's just too much of a hassle to drag the kids around."

"It's my volunteer day at Christopher's play school, so I won't be home when you come to Santa Barbara. Sorry."

My security was shaken by the new order. Now where did I fit in our mother-daughter network? I was reluctant to let go of the bond with my daughters that had sprung from my mother-of-the-bride, grandmother-of-the-newborn, position. No matter that young husbands and fathers might have sometimes felt usurped by a hovering mother-in-law! No matter that Harry and the young men of the family sometimes felt shut out by feminine chatter about reception lines and teething miseries! I wanted things to stay just like they were.

Fortunately for our entire family network—daughters and sons-in-law, husband and sons, and a young daughter still dealing with high school proms and college entrance exams—I surrendered to the inevitable and allowed myself to be pushed out of the inner circle and onto higher ground. From my new vantage point I watched proudly as my daughters became competent, independent wives and mothers who no longer needed my constant involvement in their lives.

To resist the demand for change or ignore the shifting boundaries around my daughters' lives would have threatened the peaceful alliance we had enjoyed in their nest-building years. I saw then, and have seen many times since, that I must be flexible in my relationships with my children or risk discord throughout the family.

The boundaries between generations shift as our grown children develop their own unique lifestyles. We can respond to the change as a threat or as an opportunity—a challenge to move from our peaceful plateau to higher ground. If we see change as a threat, we are in danger of slipping back onto the battlefield or beefing up our defense in a cold war. If we accept the challenge to make adjustments in our own lives, we can move forward into new territory where our relationships with our adult children will be different but even richer.

KEEPING WATCH

Maintaining the peace requires constant vigilance. In many families old issues lie dormant until some seemingly minor incident brings a recurrence of the original pain and ruffles the surface peace between generations. An immediate conflict is often resolved quickly, but deeper hurts demand further attention if restored peace is to be permanent. Otherwise, just when we grow complacent in our cease-fire status, someone may step on a long-buried land mine and the war will be on again.

QUESTIONS FOR YOU

1. What changes in family relationships did you see in the post-adolescent years? Was there a "cease-fire" period in your family? A narrowing of the generation gap?

2. Did you have difficulty finding a "peaceful plateau" with any of your children during this period? Explain.

3. How did you feel as your family nest emptied? Abandoned? Lonely? At loose ends? Challenged?

4. How do you identify the "boundaries" between you and your adult child? Which are of his making? Of yours? Mutual?

5. How do you respond to the frequent changes in your adult child's life and circumstances: Marriage? A new baby? A move?

6. Have you taken specific action to mend fences or seek peace after a misunderstanding with your adult child?

7. Where do you see pride as the culprit in your more difficult relationships?

• 5 •

Old Wounds
When Childhood Hurts Erupt

Guiding a balky cart around the holiday displays at Nielsen's market, I almost collided with my friend Ellie. We hadn't seen each other for weeks.

"I've missed you!" I said, blocking traffic in the aisle as I hugged her. "Did you and Brad have a wonderful time on your cruise?"

"Yes, we did," she answered. "But it was hard coming home. Do you have time to stop by for coffee? I need to talk."

Later we sat at her kitchen table, sharing the latest developments in our lives.

"How are things with Janet and Ryan?" I asked, after our preliminary small talk. "Are you and Janet talking again?"

Ellie poured us a second cup of coffee and pushed a plate of oatmeal cookies toward me. "That's what I wanted to talk about," she said. "So much has happened since the last time I saw you.

"Remember, I told you we were pretty sure Ryan and Janet were into drugs? And we'd made an appointment with a counselor connected with Brad's company? Well, we talked to him just before we went on vacation and decided to confront Janet with our suspicions as soon as we returned. We didn't want to start something and then take off. We were barely home and unpacked last week when Janet called to tell us that she and Ryan had separated. She dropped that bombshell as if she were announcing her latest bowling score! Brad got on the phone and demanded she come up and tell us face to face what was happening.

"It seems we were right in our suspicions, but it's Ryan who has the drug problem, according to Janet. She explained her stand-off attitude by saying she didn't want us to get involved while she was trying to 'work things out.' It would only complicate things, she said. Then she said she's always had a hard time with relationships *because of her childhood*. I just sat there with my mouth open, but Brad really hit the ceiling. He said the only thing wrong with her childhood was that she had too many advantages! He asked her who she thought she was that she could just push us aside when she felt like it. Then he got up and left the room and didn't come back until after she'd gone. He reacts that way when he's hurt, you know. I tried to smooth things over and act supportive, but she just stared after her father and shut me out."

Ellie rolled her paper napkin into a ball and dabbed at the tears that coated her dark lashes. "It's bad enough that Ryan has a drug problem, but I feel like we're losing our daughter all over again. And I don't know what Janet's childhood has to do with anything. Are we somehow to blame for her choosing to marry Ryan?

"It seems she's replaced her family with a group of strangers. She's gotten involved with this codependency thing, which is supposed to help her cope with Ryan's addiction. I can go along with that, but these people encouraged her to hook up with Adult Children of Alcoholics, of all things. We're not alcoholics, for heaven's sake! She says that's not the point, that the same principles apply to children from dysfunctional families. So now we're a dysfunctional

family! Can you believe that? Janet's changed. I don't know
what to do."

Ellie's hand trembled as she lifted her coffee cup to her
lips. I searched for words to comfort my friend, who seemed
so blameless in her daughter's unhappiness. The dysfunctional label might better apply to my own family, with its
background of alcoholism and divorce. Did that description
fit Ellie and Brad's family? Well, who could say? Some
psychologists believe that most families are dysfunctional in
one way or another.

Ellie and I had been close friends for years, but we'd
only met occasionally with our husbands, so I didn't know
Brad very well. He seemed like a nice enough guy, aside from
his tendency to give Ellie the silent treatment when he was
annoyed. I thought of Lucas, Janet's younger brother. He'd
been a handful as a kid and, from what I'd heard, hadn't
straightened out much in his late twenties. Was Lucas's
maladjustment a sign of a "dysfunctional" childhood?

Dysfunctional families, in the broadest sense, are those
that fall short of meeting the needs of every family member.
That covers a lot of families. Ten or twenty years ago, when
Ellie and I were up to our earlobes in parenting our now-
grown children, no one warned us that we weren't being
"functional" or told us that every mistake we made would
someday come back to haunt us.

I reached out and covered Ellie's quivering hand with
my own. "Maybe your only choice is to respect Janet's desire
to work things out for herself. I'm sure that will be as hard for
you as it has been for me. We've failed our kids in a lot of
areas and in far more obvious ways than you and Brad have.
Now that we're wiser and more mature and *Christians*, we'd
like to pitch in and undo the damage we either permitted or
caused in our family. You can't blame some of our kids for
not welcoming our participation with open arms, when they
see us as the ones who created the problem in the first place!

"I think they'll get beyond that, just as you and I have

gotten beyond blaming our parents for some of our hangups. We've had to work through a lot of stuff from our pasts— without groups like ACA to help us—so I guess we shouldn't expect life to be any different for our kids. Maybe the Lord keeps them growing as adults by forcing them to look back at their childhood experiences and deal with the things that hurt them. And maybe this is another growing stage for us— standing by helplessly while we watch our children deal with the things that hurt them."

And *maybe*, I thought later as I drove home, I had better listen to my own advice. In trying to comfort Ellie, I'd been looking for relief from my own pain. Pain that came from watching a daughter's battle to exorcise ghosts from her childhood—a childhood that should have been in my protective charge. Pain that came from the bitterness of a son who accused us of depriving him of support and affection in his childhood. Pain that came from watching adult children suffer from old wounds we were somehow responsible for. If there was any wisdom in the insights I'd shared with Ellie, we could both take comfort from the thought that we, too, were still growing toward maturity.

Opportunity for growth or not, this time of exposing old wounds is a hard phase of parenthood. We're forced to recognize the sins of omission and commission that flawed our parenting. Often we recognize our errors when our young adults hit thirtysomething and begin to stagger under the burdens we may have loaded on them. Some of them will limp through life without questioning the excess baggage they're carrying; others will do what Janet appears to be doing—sorting through the heavy stuff and discarding what they can. She has chosen the better way. In lightening her pack, she will be able to meet the future with new strength and vitality.

IF THE SHOE FITS

Parents of our generation have a hard time accepting the blame—expressed or implied—laid at our feet by some of our grown children. After all, we think, we did the best we knew how. Besides, we were suffering from the effects of our own childhood traumas. But while my peers and I have tended to think in the more oblique terms of "our childhood" or "the times in which we grew up," our baby-boomer generation children have narrowed the focus with merciless precision. Parents, creators of dysfunctional families, stand accused.

Melinda Blau says blaming parents for what they did or didn't do has become a national obsession. We mid-century parents raised our 76 million baby boomers in the age of psychotherapy, with the influence of Dr. Spock and the permissive, child-oriented philosophy of that era. As enlightened parents, we expected rebellion, accepted criticism, and respected their right to go into therapy to seek healing for the scars our faulty parenting had left. "The implication," Blau says, "was that somehow they could perfect themselves."[1]

Blau and other therapists are concerned about the current trend of adult children who blame their afflictions and addictions on their parents. They see a danger of adult children getting stuck in the victim mode where parent-bashing becomes an end in itself.

But let's give our children the credit they deserve for admitting their inability to cope and for having the courage to uncover the wounds that fester in their psyches. The boomers are a generation less easily satisfied—or perhaps braver— than ours. To "perfect themselves" requires an admission of imperfection. We, on the other hand, were a generation that didn't easily expose our wounds and weaknesses for fear of being looked down upon by our neighbors who seemed to have it all together. We followed the lead of our parents and kept our skeletons closeted.

No one talked about the "family secrets." Better to hide our neuroses under a cloak of normalcy than to let anyone suspect that we were dying. Better to stay away from professional help than to have people think we were crazy. Better to lose the battle of addiction than to have anyone see our cars parked at one of those "anonymous" meetings. Our fragile pride—our only defense against a demanding society—had to be preserved at all costs.

But we—the older generation—are learning. Our once-rebellious, antiestablishment baby boomers are still teaching us to loosen up and acknowledge our failures. As we watched them grow up, we were forced to choose between our fondness for appearances and acceptance of our nonconforming children with their long hair and love ballads. They made us examine and weigh the value of our own rigid standards. As adolescents, they rejected the society we'd created. As young or middle-aged adults, they're holding us responsible for the injuries our imperfect parenting inflicted upon them. If the shoe fits, we'd better put it on.

OVERKILL

Sometimes, of course, the shoe pinches more than we parents deserve. Parent bashing has become a popular pastime in recent years. Our defenders insist that most of us meant well and did the best we could under whatever circumstances we faced. One "mother who meant well" wrote to Ann Landers, looking for solace after an "emotional, guilt-laden talk" with her maladjusted adult child. Landers replied:

Dear Meant Well:

To you and the thousands of other parents who are miserable because of "what you have done" to your children, I say this: Stop beating yourselves. You did the best you could with the tools at hand—inexperience, clay feet, the works. No one knows why some children turn out to be champions in spite of parents who provided precious little emotional nourishment, while other kids— loved, wanted, tenderly nurtured, with all the so-called advantages—turn out perverse, estranged, and unable to cope.

I have come to believe in the genetic factor that has been ignored by many behavioral "experts." We all inherit our nervous systems and if the nervous system is fragile, it places severe limitations on what a person can tolerate. Certain individuals are born survivors. They can withstand life's harshest blows and emerge the stronger for it. Others crumble in the face of minor adversity. The same fire that melts butter can make steel strong.

And let us not overlook personal responsibility. I am sick of hearing children blame their parents for their messed-up lives. People with all sorts of handicaps can and do make it in this demanding and competitive world. I see evidence of this phenomenon all around me—and if you look closely, you will see it, too.

For those who are hooked on dope, there are drug-abuse centers with trained personnel, eager and waiting to help. For individuals who need professional counseling, there are mental health clinics. Self-help groups do a remarkable job—and they are free: Alcoholics Anonymous, Gamblers Anonymous, Recovery Inc. The list is endless.

Enough of this "You damaged me, now take care of me" nonsense. It's a cop-out. The parental guilt laid on by our kids is so thick you can cut it with a knife. It serves no purpose except to perpetuate financial and emotional dependence and create a climate of hostility, punishment and ultimate failure. God helps those who help themselves.[2]

Advice columnist Ann Landers has received thousands of letters from maladjusted adults who blame their inability to cope—to hold a job, maintain a relationship, and so forth—on defective parenting. She protests the excuse-making that circumvents personal responsibility. She encourages the wounded adult child to get past the "blame" cycle that is counterproductive to recovery from the past. Blame directed toward parents may be justified, but its perpetuation only serves to intensify the resentment that cripples the bearer. Landers is right in saying: "Hate and bitterness are like acid. They do more damage to the vessel in which they are stored than to the object on which they are poured.[3]

For several years Harriet and Ray have watched their son limp through life, nursing the painful wounds of his childhood but doing little to promote their healing. His parents acknowledge their responsibility for his pain, although they were unaware of his bitter feelings until recently.

"Harriet and I married when Travis was eight years old," Ray said. "We had a shared custody arrangement with his mother, my ex-wife. Travis was a quiet, amiable little kid, and I have to admit he didn't get a lot of attention. Harriet's son, Robbie, lived with us all the time, and my ex's stepdaughter lived with that family, so Travis was the only one who got bounced back and forth. You know, we thought we were doing the best thing for him with the shared custody, but I'm not so sure now. He didn't feel like he belonged anywhere. None of us had a clue of the resentment he was carrying until he was into his twenties, experimenting with drugs and having some minor run-ins with the law.

"When the court ordered counseling as a condition of his probation, all hell broke loose. That's when he zeroed in on his underprivileged childhood as the cause of everything that had ever gone wrong in his life. He withdrew from all of us for a while, but lately he's established some sort of relationship with his mother again. I think she assumes, like Travis, that I did most of the neglecting and gives him the sympathy he's looking for. What he really needs is to take responsibility for where he is now and stop feeling sorry for himself.

"I'm truly sorry for my part in his misery and I've told him so. But I guess it's too late. He goes around telling people that his father isn't part of his life anymore."

Travis's estrangement from his father is helping to keep

him an emotional cripple, stuck in the role of victim. He needs professional guidance in getting in touch with feelings that took root at a sensitive age and grew in silence for twenty years. He needs to be willing to work toward forgiveness and truth.

LOOKING FOR TRUTH

Thirty-five-year-old Midge came from a family whose system was built on pretense and denial. To the community they were exemplary. At home, behind closed doors, Midge and her siblings were terrorized by their father's physical and emotional abuse and bewildered by their mother's apparent lack of concern.

"I used to think how phony we were when we all filed into church on Sunday morning," Midge said. "Dad was an elder and Mom a deacon—pillars of the congregation, you might say. Everyone thought they were wonderful. I did, too, in a way. Some of the attention they got rubbed off on us kids.

"After church we'd go to the local diner for lunch. Our parents usually had some 'poor, suffering soul'—my mother's words—under their wings. The adults would sit at one end of the table talking in hushed tones about whatever the current crisis was and we kids would sit at the other, wanting to get home to be with our friends or whatever. Unless, of course, we'd get Dad's delayed reaction to something one of us had done or not done in church. It wasn't unusual for him to fly into a rage about something as soon as we hit the front hall. Then he'd yell and Mother would escape to the kitchen to cry. He might start beating on one of my brothers or he might just storm around for a while. In either case, my reaction would be to go and sit in the kitchen with my mother. I never knew what to say, because she always pretended nothing was really wrong—she was crying for the friend we'd taken to lunch or because she had a headache or something. *No one would ever talk about what was really going on!*"

Midge and her siblings grew up feeling robbed of the kind of love and attention they saw outsiders receiving. Each learned to play a role that helped him or her cope with the situation on the home front.

"My older sister turned everything inward, I tried to make peace, and my brothers rebelled by getting into drugs and alcohol. Every one of us has had a struggle as an adult because of the unresolved issues of our crazy childhood.

"I didn't put all this together until a few years ago when a personal crisis forced me to go for counseling. Since then I've discovered that my sister is bulimic, one brother has been in and out of treatment centers for drug and alcohol addiction, and the other was recently arrested for assault and battery. If my parents know all this, they ignore it. They go on pretending that theirs is the perfect family. It has nothing to do with truth."

I'd begun our informal interview by asking Midge about her relationship with her parents. Looking at the wholesome, smiling, all-American-girl image my young friend projected, I couldn't have guessed she'd come from anything but the most stable background. What surprised me as we talked was her lack of bitterness for her parents' past behavior. Her resentment was directed toward the lack of honesty in her present relationship with them.

"I need to be allowed to talk about the things that hurt me as a child," Midge said, "but Mom and Dad have been covering up for too long. They act as if none of it ever happened. They invariably bring up the dysfunctional families that they are still ministering to. 'You don't know what trouble is,' they'll say. 'If you'd had the Halliburtons for parents, you'd have something to complain about.'

"I've learned to see my parents as fallible people now, and I think I could forgive them anything if they would just acknowledge my feelings. But I can't get through to them. I truly want a close relationship with Mom and Dad, and I intend to keep trying to break through the veneer."

BURIED LAND MINES

As with Midge, whatever psychological and relational injuries children suffered in their families of origin are apt to surface in the midst of a midlife crisis. Previously, as they left the family nest and built their own, their wounds were covered or ignored. They embarked upon careers, married, and had children, often thinking they had the world by the tail—until suddenly everything seemed to come apart at the seams. Physically ill or emotionally paralyzed, they looked for causes, ripping away the temporary Band-Aids of their youth to expose festering wounds.

Sometimes healing demands extensive surgery to dig out the shrapnel of forgotten memories. In the midst of their pain, our children are understandably angry at those who failed to protect them on the battlefields of their childhood. A little parent bashing may be therapeutic. In Brenda's case "bashing" was a necessary part of her healing.

Wes and Brenda sat quietly before their pastor as he prayed for them at the beginning of an hour-long counseling session. It was no use, Brenda thought. Their marriage was as good as over. Brenda dreaded today's session. Last week Pastor Michael had asked about her family of origin, her parents' divorce, and her mother's remarriage to Brenda's stepfather, Al.

Her mind recoiled at the thought of her stepfather. She hadn't seen him in years, and she didn't want to waste time talking about him. They were supposed to be working on the marriage problems, which were mostly in Wes's imagination. He wanted more from her than she had to give, and she was just too tired to try anymore.

Pastor Michael watched the young couple with curiosity. Wes had one arm around the back of Brenda's chair. When his hand touched his wife's shoulder, she stiffened and pulled away. Wes's other hand rested on his knee, rubbing back and forth against the coarse fabric of his jeans. He looked at the pastor expectantly. Brenda clutched the purse in her lap with both hands, her eyes directed at the door or at the wall behind the pastor's head. She hadn't met his eyes since she had entered the room. It didn't take a lot of training to identify this young wife's resistance. And last week, when he'd asked about the stepfather . . .

That land mine, buried years before, was the root cause of Brenda's marital problems. She had deeply buried memories of sexual abuse and shame, and by painful probing the land mine was unearthed—and exploded. Only then could she and Wes, with professional help, walk through the fire together and come out whole. Part of her healing process was to transfer the guilt she subconsciously placed on herself to the shoulders of the man who had abused her.

Little children have no choice but to accept whatever treatment they receive. They learn to survive by burying their painful wounds under layers of denial, where they fester until the infection grows and demands exposure.

PERMANENT SCARS

"I've heard about women who manage to shove all their ugly memories into their subconscious," Daphne says. "Well, I envy them. I've never had a moment's peace from mine. I even dream about the things that happened."

As a teenager, Daphne, also abused by a stepfather, had been taken in by a sympathetic aunt. Over the years, Daphne's heart hardened against her natural mother, who had never believed Daphne's horror stories. "I hated her for not believing the truth and helping me," said Daphne, who refused to see or speak to her mother for several years. "I thought for sure God would condemn me for my hatred."

But when Daphne married Clayton, love softened her heart toward the whole world, even her mother. Her young husband encouraged Daphne to reestablish a relationship with her mother, so they went together to visit the woman.

"I thought she would greet me with open arms," Daphne said. "I was so happy with Clayton and thrilled to be pregnant with our first child. I had this fantasy of sharing my wonderful new life with my mother. I could picture us crying in each other's arms. I could almost hear Mama begging me to forgive her and I was ready. It didn't happen that way."

Daphne's voice trembled as she continued her story. "When we finally found the house where she was living—a real dump on the edge of town—the door was open and she was sitting at the kitchen table playing cards with a couple of scroungy-looking buddies.

" 'Hello, Mama,' I said.

" 'Oh, it's you,' she said, hardly glancing up. 'C'mon in.' Then she went back to laughing and talking with her friends.

"Clayton and I stood there inside the doorway for at least ten minutes, waiting for someone to do something, but they just went on playing cards. No open arms, no tears, no forgiveness. By the time Clayton tugged on my arm to leave, all the old hatred had boiled up inside me again. I swore that was the last time I'd set myself up for a fall. It hurt bad at the time." Daphne shrugged her shoulders and brushed a stray lock of blond hair from her forehead. Her voice was steady again. "But that was fifteen years ago. I don't care anymore. I really don't. I don't hate her. I consider her dead."

Daphne may not have buried her memories, but for fifteen years she has buried both her hope and her throbbing hatred behind a fortress of indifference.

Daphne began her life trusting her mother to meet her needs. She needed protection, she needed to be believed, she needed to be cared for. Her mother betrayed her daughter's trust at every turn. Daphne will bear the scars of rejection all of her life.

SHIFTING BURDENS

Where some parents deliberately and cruelly inflict physical or emotional injury upon those they are supposed to protect, many more unwittingly pass on family codes and patterns that burden their children in more subtle ways.

Wanda is a case in point: "My mother gave me her snobbishness just as surely as she gave me her brown eyes," she said. "I realize now that her attitudes came out of her own inferiority complex, but she transferred them to me so well that I had no basis for judging people except by their social or economic standing. If a boy lived on the east side of town, I knew that Mom would be less than enthusiastic about my bringing him home. Oh, she would be kind and polite, but she wouldn't gush like she did when I brought home a guy who lived on the hill and whose dad was an attorney. I not only learned to judge others by my mother's standards, I judged myself the same way. When I grew up and married a professional man, lived in one of the best neighborhoods, and ran around town in a Mercedes—things that my mother bragged about to her friends—I expected to feel really good about myself. But I didn't.

"A healthy bank account couldn't prevent my alcoholism or the state of spiritual bankruptcy that I finally came to. It took involvement with a group of people suffering from the same addiction as I and a lot of therapy before I began to question and reorganize my personal values. You know, those anonymous self-help groups are wonderful. You don't know if Jim W. is a laborer or lawyer until you've developed a sincere respect for him as a human being, and then you see it doesn't matter.

"I'd never really *known* anyone from the wrong side of the tracks before. I can't tell you what an eye-opener that was. Even so, I had a hard time shaking my priggishness and discovering who I was underneath it all. I hadn't had any values of my own before, because I'd taken on the ones that my mother had bequeathed to me. When I realized that, I rebelled like an angry teenager. Here I was, thirty-three years old and all screwed up because I'd been an innocent victim of my mom's phony value system. I didn't stop to think that my brother had grown up in the same household and was a pretty stable character. I needed someone to blame for my problems."

Wanda had identified closely with her mother and like a sponge absorbed her attitudes. But the sponge eventually became too heavy to carry around. She didn't recognize her false values as burdens to be discarded until alcoholism and divorce shattered her complacency.

"For the first few years of recovery from my illness, I resented Mom for the legacy she'd passed on to me. I saw her as a snob and a bigot, and I felt very superior for having learned what was truly important in life. Everything I did flew in the face of her convictions, some of which were pure as gold. She was embarrassed by the change in me. I thought, mistakenly, she would have preferred me to continue my closet drinking than to declare myself an alcoholic. I thought she would rather see me in a bad marriage than wear the stigma of divorce. Our relationship went downhill for several years while I nursed a large grudge and she nursed her wounded feelings.

"A significant part of my recovery program involved belief that a Higher Power could restore me to sanity and serenity and help me to grow spiritually. My bitterness and resentment were inconsistent with those goals and eventually I had to give them up. I had to allow my mother the right to her humanness and forgive her. She had many sterling qualities as a mother, and she certainly did the best she could with what she had to work with. We both mellowed out and had a pretty good friendship going during the last years of her life. I'm glad for that.

"I'd like things to be different between me and my girls when they grow up, but I know I've passed on some garbage to them—probably still do. They'll probably wind up in one of those Adult Children of Alcoholics groups and resent me for the things I've done to them. I see what God means about the 'sins of the fathers' being passed on to the fourth generation!"

Wanda's parents weren't abusive. Her father was a highly successful businessman who proudly moved his family into a prestigious neighborhood. Like other fathers of his generation, he left child raising and all other domestic matters to his wife while he worked long hours to maintain his hold on their achieved standard of living. Her mother, who had not been raised in a privileged home, tried hard to fit into a segment of society foreign to her. As she watched closely to see how her neighbors dressed their children, decorated their homes, and entertained their friends, she developed a strategy for survival that she passed on to her children. Wanda absorbed her mother's insecurity along with her standards for behavior.

A TIME OF HEALING

Most adult children come to a place where they need to drop some of the excess baggage handed them by their parents. They will recognize the fallacy of some of the messages, rules, and attitudes carried into adulthood from their families of origin. An early stage of this "unloading" is resentment, and if and when we parents find ourselves on the receiving end of this resentment, we need to understand what is happening.

If our children feel free to be open and honest with us, we are almost guaranteed a confrontation about past errors in our parenting. Know that such confrontation, however hostile, takes courage. We can react defensively (grabbing those shields of pride for protection) or we can embrace every opportunity to help heal the old wounds that mar our relationships with our adult children.

In the process of confronting and working through the false values she'd brought from childhood, Wanda went from resenting her mother to understanding and forgiving her. Her mother played a part in Wanda's progress by respecting her daughter's efforts to recover from addiction, by listening to Wanda's accusations, and by acknowledging her own insecurity.

"When I began to see my mother as a frightened young woman instead of a powerful adult—when I began to see her as a person and not just a parent—it was easy to forgive her. As we shared our deep feelings, I saw that the attitudes she'd brought from her family of origin had affected her approach to everything. My mother passed on the rules that she thought would help me to 'fit in,' a goal that seemed of utmost importance to her."

Brenda's struggle to recover from her past was more difficult. Her failing marriage had driven her to a place where she needed to look at her background of abuse. She resisted exposing and reliving her terrible memories and feeling the guilt and shame that accompanied them. With the gentle guidance of a professional, she is still working through her anger and grief to a point of acceptance and detachment from her past. "There is light at the end of the tunnel," she says.

Some members of Brenda's family of origin have supported her as she revealed the sordid details of her childhood. "The most important thing they did for me was believe me and share in my rage. My mother, long divorced from the monster in my memories, was devastated at the realization that she might have protected me. But she didn't know what was happening. She'd come from a pretty awful background herself, and she didn't have the skills to cope with marriage or motherhood. She's grown by leaps and bounds since my childhood, and we're developing a whole new relationship. It's one of the small bonuses that makes this painful recovery process worthwhile."

The testimonies of these young women can give us valuable direction as we become aware that our adult children are working through the unavoidable pains of the past. As parents, we have a choice in how we will respond when and if an adult child confronts us with the evidence of a wounded childhood.

We can deny that any wounds exist: "Jennifer's counselor has her digging into the past for reasons for her bulimia, when anyone who knows us could tell you that she had the most normal childhood ever!"

We can pass the buck: "It was that modeling job that got her obsessed with losing weight. She certainly didn't get the notion from us."

Or we can acknowledge our responsibility for whatever role we might have played in her present dilemma and become allies in her battle for wholeness.

That's what Ellie and Brad did for their daughter, Janet. In spite of Janet's cool, sometimes hostile, attitude, they wanted to help her in any way they could. They swallowed their initial resentment because they cared more about Janet's well-being than about any perfect-parent illusions they might have had. They continued their counseling, shifting their focus from Janet and her problems to themselves as parents and looking for some of the dysfunctional patterns that had characterized their family system. They accepted Janet's standoffishness, maintaining their ties to their grandchildren and keeping the doors of communication open for a time when Janet might turn to them. As Ellie and Brad became healthier as a couple, they were strong allies in Janet's struggle to put her life back together.

"It was hard for all of us," Ellie said. "But it was worth it."

OPEN HEARTS

Like Ellie and Brad, most of us did the best we could at the job of parenting. Our children were hurt in spite of us and, at times, because of us. Many of these hurts heal over and cause no further problems, but some old wounds will surface in later years to demand attention. When that happens, we parents need to open our hearts in compassion for the pain our children express.

It is easy to be openhearted when we are secure in someone's love, when that person accepts us as we are. God does that for us and prompts us to do the same for one another. But how shall we open our hearts when we, too, have been wounded in action? As our children have been wounded by our blunders, we have been hurt by their rebellion and rejection—and now by their accusations of abuse and neglect. It will take courage and humility to be openhearted.

We have a choice. Closed hearts may protect us from further injury, but they will also block the communication that can heal old wounds and provide a new foundation for rebonding.

Open hearts require open minds willing to listen to adult children and acknowledge their feelings and grievances, no matter how unfounded they may seem. Open hearts demonstrate a willingness to be flexible and to look at circumstances through another's eyes.

As your adult children seek healing from the old wounds that cripple their current lives, listen with compassion. Try to step back and see their view, acknowledging your mistakes, asking for forgiveness, reassuring them of your love and support. Do your part, let God manage the healing, and you can begin to enjoy a new and closer relationship with your adult child.

QUESTIONS FOR YOU

1. Dysfunctional families are those that fall short of meeting the needs of every member. In what areas, if any, might your family have been dysfunctional while your children were growing up?

2. What "wounds" do you think your son or daughter might have sustained during childhood?

3. Can you identify unresolved issues from your own family of origin that you might have passed on to your child? If so, what are they? How do they affect his or her adult life?

4. Has an adult child ever held you responsible or confronted you with blame for the problems in his or her life? How do you feel about it? Hurt? Guilty? Misunderstood? Remorseful?

5. How can you help your child heal from the childhood wounds as they come to the surface?

6. Have you taken the steps suggested in the last paragraph so that you and your adult child can move on toward a closer relationship?

• 6 •

Reconnaissance
Finding New Grounds for Relationship

Having survived the turbulence of adolescent rebellion and the conflicts and confrontations of the years that followed, parents yearn for a peaceful coexistence with their adult children. Finding a common ground for relationship can be hard, with each generation engaged in battles on different fronts.

A mother faces the mysteries of menopause while her daughter juggles a career with the demands of motherhood. A father braces for retirement and the unknowns of the future while his son tries to find his niche in the business world. Crises can happen to a parent in his fifties or sixties as well as to a thirtysomething child. Sometimes we are so entangled in the challenge of the moment that our most significant relationships threaten to dissolve into insignificance.

In the cease-fire period that followed the breaking away of our young adults, we were happy allies together, sharing the adventure of expanding family boundaries. We parents were still at the center of things, secure in our familiar place as parents. But in the natural course of events, the generation gap widened again, and we became two families—or three or four—instead of one.

Life demands change. Our children leave home, marry, have babies, sometimes divorce or become ill or widowed; we maintain the family home or move to a smaller one, beome ill or widowed, sometimes even divorce. Each of these milestones changes our relationship with our grown children. Each of these milestones changes *us*. We parents are most threatened by change, because we feel responsible for maintaining the family equilibrium. We can do battle with the life-cycle circumstances that bring about changes in our system, but we can't hope to win. We will either shift position and allow for reorganization or we will end up with no family system—no relationship—at all.

BREAKING PATTERNS

Ellie and I met again for lunch.

"I'm not sure where we are in our relationship with Janet, except that we're all changing," she said. "I feel like one of those lobsters we studied in Biology 101, remember?"

I remembered. We'd watched a captive lobster as it grew, periodically shedding its hard shell during the growth stages. A soft new shell formed inside the old and expanded to a larger size before it slowly hardened. While it was soft, though, the poor defenseless creature would hide in its burrow in the aquarium.

"Brad and I are in that soft-shelled phase," Ellie continued. "We're trying to find where we fit in Janet's life while she's working through her own problems. We've taken off our hard-shell parenting role, and we're trying to grow into whatever role God has for us next. Janet's vulnerable too, of course, so we're very careful about how we approach her these days."

Ellie talked about some of the things she and Brad were learning through their counseling sessions.

"Mr. Woods, our counselor, said we'd been 'triangling.' He said there was tension between Brad and me, and because of that, we had a need to bring Janet into our relationship. He said we'd never learned how to be a couple after Janet left home. When she was away at school, we were either planning a trip to visit her or setting the stage for her next homecoming. We've triangled with Lucas, too, to some extent, but he doesn't cooperate by staying in place for long! So we keep drawing Janet back into our triangle. Even on our cruise, conversation about Janet took priority over everything else. Brad confessed that he was a little disappointed in our vacation; he thought it would be a chance for us to get closer. I had no idea he felt that way.

"Parenting is a hard habit to break," Ellie continued, "even when we can see that pulling back is the best strategy. There's always this nagging idea in the back of your mind that you can help somehow. And of course we have a right to try, but we need to know when to step aside. The thing is, we saw that we'd been fighting to hang on to Janet partly for our benefit, not just for hers. We're working on breaking that triangle pattern."

As their counseling continued, Ellie and Brad began to see how they'd allowed Janet to feel responsible for their happiness. Janet had always been the "good" daughter— bringing home the A's, winning the scholastic awards, volunteering for community service, and generally making them proud. She was continual proof that they were "good" parents, in spite of her rebellious brother, Lucas.

Ryan's drug addiction caused Janet to withdraw from her parents rather than risk their disappointment by revealing a flaw in her pristine record. But as she watched her parents begin to focus on themselves and each other rather than on her and her family, Janet was freed to make choices based on her own needs, not theirs. If her marriage were to fail, it would be a tragedy for her and the children. She didn't need the added burden of having ruined her parents' lives.

Ellie shared more insights as time went on.

"Apparently we've been stalled in our parenting role

because it's familiar and comfortable and because we haven't known where to go from here. Brad's parents both died in their sixties. My father died when I was in my teens and Mom has been handicapped by one illness or another for most of my adult years. So we've been without personal role models for this time of life. It's like there *isn't* any life after parenting."

Ellie's and my generation is youth-centered. Our baby-boomer children, by sheer numbers, command the attention of American business and popular culture. Perhaps we older adults have a subconscious desire to remain closely involved with them in order to absorb their vitality. But somewhere along the line they will resist our involvement, and we will have to find our own vitality. That's what Ellie and Brad are doing.

A NEW TEAM

Before we can reorganize our family system, we have to *reconnoiter*—take stock of where we are and what resources we have.

"We're beginning to learn who we are as a couple now," Ellie continued. "And we appreciate the fact that we *are* still a couple when so many of our friends are divorced. We're certainly not the same two youngsters who married right out of college, so we can't find ourselves by regressing to that stage of our lives. We have to take inventory of our strengths and weaknesses as a couple and as individuals. We have to explore some reasons for living outside and beyond our children. It's quite an adventure."

Professionals affirm that necessity:

We can make our lives good or we can make our lives bad when the kids are gone. We can reacquaint ourselves with who we are besides Mommy and Daddy, or we can feel empty as our roles of twenty-odd years are lost and our identities with them. We can blame our being at sea

• 97 •

on each other, or we can come together to form a new team with a new agenda. We can experiment with our new relative freedom or we can go lock step together toward whatever it is we think we see at the end of the road.[1]

To "form a new team with a new agenda," the marriage bond—our primary earthly relationship—may need to be resurrected and dusted off. Conflict with adolescents and young adults can be hard on a marriage. Now, with the children grown and less dependent upon us, we have time to rekindle the spark that began our family system in the first place.

Falling in love again brings new vitality into the marriage bond. It helps us to see ourselves as individuals outside of our parenting roles. A husband can thrive as he once again becomes the center of his wife's attention. A wife, mirrored by the renewed love in her partner's eyes, can begin to value herself as a woman, and not just as a mother.

I experienced this personally when the last of our children left home. Harry and I heaved a huge sigh of relief that we'd come through the "blending" years with our marriage and sanity intact. For the first time in a dozen years we found time to focus on each other and look ahead to a life that didn't revolve exclusively around our children.

"Aren't you just rattling around in that big house now?" a neighbor asked. "Chad and I don't know what to do with ourselves since Kim and Corrine went off to college."

An acquaintance watching me buy a beef roast at the local meat market asked, "Isn't it hard to learn to cook for two again after so many years of feeding a family? I invariably cook too much and don't know what to do with the leftovers."

I smiled and nodded in sympathy, but felt like a hypocrite; I was embarrassed to admit that I thoroughly enjoyed the new life Harry and I were discovering as a couple. We'd missed the conventional preparental honeymoon period. In the first few months of our marriage, we'd been crammed into a three-bedroom house with wall-to-wall children and neither bedroom nor closet space to call our own! We were happy enough now to "rattle around" for a change. As for the leftovers, one night's roast meant two future nights of freedom from "scratch" cooking that had occupied so many hours of my past days.

Only the grace of God carried us through the dozen crazy, wonderful, overwhelming years that followed our marriage. On a good day I'd thrived on it; on a bad day I'd dragged out the hidden calendar that marked off the years until the last child would graduate from high school. Now we were experiencing the comparative tranquility that I'd only fantasized about.

Gail Sheehy has made an interesting observation:

> The women who go off the charts in happiness are middle-aged; just past menopause; friends with, but unconfined by, their now grown children; and feeling a firm sense of their own identity for the first time. In general, being older correlates with being less bored, less lonely, more in control of one's inner needs and outer environment and more likely to report no major fears.[2]

The possibilities for filling the active-parenting void are endless, limited only by health and finances. Sheehy paints a positive picture of "life after children:"

> By middle age we know pretty well what we can and cannot do, which roles are essential to maintaining our core identity and which roles we can outlive. But probably few of us are aware of the new potentials and special strengths released between 45 and 60 that are *exclusive* to middle age.
>
> • relaxation of roles
> • greater assertiveness in women
> • greater expressiveness in men
> • being free to say what you think
> • being free to pick up and go, again

- more time and money for yourself
- more tolerance for others
- greater opportunities for companionship with your mate
- chance to meet your children again as friends
- possibility for contributing to your community, your history, your culture.[3]

There's an old adage I like that says God never closes a door without opening a window. As we meet the challenge of change and distance ourselves from our parenting roles, we will discover new vistas of possibility and new dimensions in our relationships. We are not asked to forfeit our relationships with our adult children, only to modify them to fit our changing circumstances.

Like many women of my generation, I'd invested myself almost totally in homemaking and mothering. I was unsure of my ability to learn any other role. In my nearsighted youth I'd assumed that life beyond fifty was a dreary downhill slide anyway. Now, seeing the intriguing possibilities beyond the emptying of the nest, a whole new world opened up to me. I could begin to release my grip on my children when I didn't need their dependence to justify my existence.

Because Harry's professional life continued as before, his release from active parenting was somewhat less dramatic than mine. Even so, the pressure was off. For years he'd struggled to provide an income sufficient for the needs of our large family, watching our expenses increase faster than the profits from his successful business. Now, in our empty-nest life, he could browse through the travel folders or drive slowly by the new cars in the display window at Sun Motors. Where he'd battled with our teens over the cost of lights left burning and gas wasted in unnecessary trips to town, he now had the freedom to be generous, to stop a retreating visitor with, "You'd better take a few dollars in case you need something extra this week."

Writing from the perspective of an adult child, Harold Ivan Smith reassures us: "Scripture does not call for an amputation of parental ties, but for gradual emancipation from them."[4] We are called to do our part by releasing our children to independence and seeking an independence of our own. We can help our adult children most by demonstrating our confidence in them as mature people who are capable of fighting their own battles.

A NEW STAGE OF PARENTHOOD

Jerry and Mary White say that growth into independence is a process for both parents and young adults. "Growth never moves forward evenly," they write, "but by leaps and spurts with intermittent periods of tranquility." They describe parents as needing to move through four distinct stages of parenthood:

- *controlling*, using authority to direct and protect;
- *coaching*, guiding, teaching, and correcting;
- *counseling*, giving advice with no strings attached; and
- *caring*.

Caring is the culmination of a successful process of parenting adult children. You care, you love—not demanding anything in return. Your adult offspring recognize your care and concern and respond to it with respect and honor. At times they ask for this care to be expressed in counsel or in coaching. But we initiate neither, allowing them the total freedom of choice. We now impact their lives on the basis of love and influence.[5]

So we are left with love. There's a Greek word, *storge*, for the special love of parent for child. God gives parents the gift of *storge* love so his helpless human creatures will be protected and nurtured into maturity. C. S. Lewis calls this variety of natural love the "most humble and widely diffused" of all.[6] That we too easily twist and corrupt such a love is a sad symptom of our humanity.

Only by God's light can we see the temptation to corrupt our maternal/paternal love. We loudly demand or quietly expect our children's allegiance, whether or not we've earned it. Being needed by our children is *our* need. Many of us, especially mothers of my generation, have found our greatest fulfillment in our maternal role. It's hard to let go. But God has a new assignment for us.

We have been transferred to a rear-guard position. This is the new ground upon which we can build a new kind of relationship. We can still impact our children's lives on the basis of love and influence.

LOVING GOD'S WAY

Learning how to love in a hands-off way is the challenge. If we are in doubt about how to demonstrate our parental love to our grown children, we can be guided by looking at a portion of the biblical love chapter: 1 Corinthians 13.

> Love is patient, love is kind. It does not envy, it does not boast, it is not proud. It is not rude, it is not self-seeking, it is not easily angered, it keeps no record of wrongs. Love does not delight in evil but rejoices with the truth. It always protects, always trusts, always hopes, always perseveres. Love never fails. (1 Cor. 13:4–8)

Love is patient. *Longsuffering* is the word used by some Bible translations. Mother-martyrs readily identify with that term, but God doesn't call us to wrap ourselves in martyrdom. Instead he offers us his power to endure the suffering that will inevitably accompany loving other human beings. To love is to be vulnerable. We are bound to be hurt sometimes—either *by* the ones we love or by standing *with* them in the line of fire from their enemies.

As our children tear at the ties that bind them to us, we will suffer. They will reject our advice, confront us with forgotten sins of omission and commission, and turn to others for the help we long to give. Patient love comes from a waiting heart. Patient love enables us to return to the front lines after feeling the sting of battle.

Love is kind. To be kind is to be considerate. We will consider the feelings of the ones we love, taking our eyes off our own injuries and tending to theirs—if they'll let us. We will consider their circumstances, put ourselves in their shoes, and look at the world through their eyes. To be kind is to be benevolent, giving of ourselves even when there is nothing in it for us.

Parental love for a newborn appears to be kindness itself. We are sacrificing servants to our infants' needs. Ego-building rewards of unquestioning devotion kept us going through sleepless, colicky nights. But true kindness builds another's ego, not our own. When our children fail to show their devotion, will we still be kind? Can we reach out in healing love with no expectation of reward?

Love does not envy, it does not boast, it is not proud. Love reaches out toward the beloved. Envy turns us inward again, aware of what we lack, diminished somehow by another's success. Prideful boasting, an outgrowth of envy, can be an attempt to puff ourselves up against the threat of insignificance.

When our children achieve what we haven't given them, we feel a twinge of uneasiness. They have withdrawn their neediness from us. They are not giving us credit. "My daughter, the doctor," we say to our friends, hoping her light will shine on us. Love without envy rejoices at my child's success for *her* sake, not mine.

Love is not rude. Rudeness assumes the liberty to be discourteous. Ridicule and sarcasm are inconsistent with love, which does not ignore the rules of polite behavior. It does not give to a stranger what it denies the beloved.

Secure in our family circles, we speak our minds: "Now don't take offense, but . . ." Our family will understand, we think, as we tread upon their sensitive toes with jibes of criticism. We mean to help, we insist, as our adult children shield themselves from our friendly fire.

Love is not self-seeking. Love is self-forgetful, seeking the highest good for the beloved. Surprise fringe benefits reward our self-forgetfulness. If they are *not* a surprise, our selfless love is corrupted! Self-knowledge and self-fulfillment are important, but when God assigns us to an inward journey, he will conduct the search.

I will have to wrench myself away from seeking my reason for being in my adult children. God allowed me to be immersed and content in the nurturing role of young motherhood, but it was for love's purpose. To make my adult children responsible for my fulfillment is to drag them backward.

Love is not easily angered. The psalmist gives us our model in his description of God: "slow to anger, abounding in love and faithfulness" (Ps. 86:15). Therein lies our holy example. There is no room for touchiness or irritability in love.

Anger is a proper response to evil and injustice in the world and in our relationships. But when our adult children hurt us with rejection or accusations of past wrongs, an angry reaction will only exacerbate the problem.

Love keeps no record of wrongs. Love is not grudge-bearing. It does not stockpile the faults and misdeeds of the beloved like ammunition to be used in the next conflict. It has no desire for revenge or self-justification. Love forgives and lays aside resentment.

If we are misunderstood or unappreciated by our adult children, our feelings are hurt. Our temptation is to nurse our small grudges with the milk of self-pity until they grow into full-grown resentments, which take on lives of their own and crowd out love. Resentment darkens our dispositions and drives our children further away; feeling the pain of rejection, we want to retaliate. Eventually a word or an act will tip the scales of self-control; we drag out the ammunition we've been collecting and let fly.

There is a time for healthy confrontation, but it must be in an atmosphere of love with the intention of healing, not fueled by resentment, so often characterized by, "Oh, I know you didn't mean it, but . . ." or "You probably didn't realize it, but . . ."

Love does not delight in evil, but rejoices with the truth. Evil is the other side of love's coin. It is the wrong that causes God's people to suffer and to bring suffering to one another. Evil slinks into our everyday world on Satan's lies. Jesus came in love to arm us against the lies of the Evil One. He repeatedly said, "I tell you the truth." At one point he declared: "I am the truth" (John 14:6).

Too often, just when we think the love we have for our children is pure, without the taint of evil, we find ourselves corrupting our love with impatience, unkindness, envy, rudeness, resentment—allowing the enemies of love to infiltrate the boundaries of our love relationships. Truth will stand against these enemies, as we seek to be transparently honest in our dealings with them.

Love always protects, always trusts, always hopes, always perseveres. Love is the fortress that surrounds and protects our relationships. It is the armor that shields our human love bond from the flaming arrows of mistrust and misunderstanding. Love is an optimistic warrior, "joyful in hope, patient in affliction, faithful in prayer" (Rom. 12:12).

As our children fight for the freedom of independence, we mourn our losses. Our relationships with them undergo radical change, and we don't know where we stand. God directs us to function within the boundaries of love, to trust in him and his guidance toward a new connection. He is our role model of faithful love, demonstrating in his love for us a new way to love our adult children. We will have to sweep away our pride and our petulance.

Love never fails. Love will survive, in spite of our

human failure. God's love is eternal and will never be withdrawn from us, although every earthly relationship may falter and die. His love is the power to heal and restore, to endure the pain of human love and to persevere in hope.

"Love each other as I have loved you," Jesus said (John 15:12). The words are not a suggestion, but a command. Our grown children may ignore, mistreat, or reject us, but we are to love them. They may hurt our feelings, but we are to love them. We fight to restore broken bonds and are defeated by anger and resentment. We'd rather withdraw from battle than risk further hurt. We'd rather stop loving the children we've loved, but God says we are to love them.

"As I have loved you," he said. He wants us to love one another with a divine love, the *agape* love that led the Father to give his one and only Son for our eternal salvation. God does not ask us for the impossible; we can do all things in his strength (Phil. 4:13). So it's with the power of God's love for me that I can love my son who has rejected me as a mother. I don't feel like it. Rejection hurts. Hurt becomes anger and freezes into resentment. My love has failed. No matter. God knew it would. His love is unwavering and indestructible, waiting to heal and restore.

Too often human love fails to protect the parent-child bond that God entrusted to our care. Adult children turn their backs on their parents, and parents sever relationships with their adult children. As Christians we know that God's heart grieves to see the corruption of love on both sides of our disconnected relationship. He reaches out with the power of his agape love, promising his faithful guidance and protection.

Divine love will surround us and follow us into eternity. This love gently prods us to love one another. We have given our children care and been rewarded with their devotion; we have given them counsel and been rewarded, sometimes, by their victories. When care is outgrown and counsel is rejected, we are left with love. Human love wants to be rewarded for its efforts, but God's love desires nothing besides the comfort and joy of the beloved. In God's strength we can align our goals with his and meet the challenge of loving relationships with our adult children.

THE GIFT OF EXAMPLE

As we settle for relationships with our grown children based on loving and not on directing, as we grant them their rightful independence and relinquish our positions of power, we have an opportunity to influence them in a new way. We may no longer be able to fix their lives, but we can fix our own. We are never too old to examine our value systems and our attitudes and to change what needs changing.

Most of us are led to make changes in ourselves and our lifestyles in order to achieve a balance in our empty-nest years. In Ellie and Brad's life, Janet had been like the third leg of a three-legged stool. When she pulled away from her parents, their family system was thrown off balance. If their daughter had allowed it, they would have attempted to restore the old order by focusing on her, but because she held them at a distance, they were forced to take stock of their own resources as individuals and as a couple. In the long run, the adjustments Ellie and Brad made strengthened the family system of which Janet and her children were still very much a part.

Arthur Maslow and Moira Duggan have good advice for us all:

The most helpful thing they [parents] can do is to demonstrate to their children that they themselves are capable *at any point in their lives* of changing, of adding to their experience, of doing things differently from before. Even if they try to conceal the darker side of their lives— the fears and imperfections and shortcomings we all have in some measure—their children will see through to the truth. Our power to shape our children's lives lies in the power we have to shape our own lives and in so doing to be role models for them (not necessarily images of perfection).[8]

Probably the most loving thing we can do for our adult children is to walk through life before them as trailblazers. We can give them a love gift of example as we meet the challenge of changing circumstance.

We can model flexibility.

I met my friend Kay at a college extension course for creative writers. She had come to Santa Barbara as a seventy-year-old widow, rented an apartment, and bought a small business, which she operated until she tired of having to get up so early in the morning. At eighty-four she sold her shop, retired, and resumed work on a book about her earlier years in the movie industry. She was pushing ninety when she bought her computer and learned to use the word processor. In her "spare" time she volunteered as a docent at the art museum and stuffed envelopes for her political party.

In response to my awe of her energy, she insisted that her good health enabled her to resist the pull of the rocking chair. But at ninety she suffered two broken verterbrae lugging a basket of wet laundry up her apartment stairs. After several months in the hospital and convalescent home, she was back at her writing.

Recently she had to leave the apartment she loved because it was being restored as a historical landmark. Undaunted, she found an apartment across town (no small challenge in Santa Barbara), rented a U-Haul truck, and hired two men from the unemployment office to move her again. At ninety-two she keeps busy writing, researching, and submitting her work to various editors. Last Christmas she drove her little Honda to visit her son in the Bay Area, about four hundred miles north. Kay is flexibility personified, and has been an inspiration to me in the years I've known her. That's the kind of trailblazing I'd like to do for my children as I get older.

We can model enthusiasm.

One crisp autumn night Harry and I joined fellow Elderhostelers—those aging people who sign up and travel to various college campuses to take noncredit courses specifically designed for them—for orientation at Feather River College in California. Maude and Otis stood to introduce themselves. "Is this your first Elderhostel?" our young activity coordinator asked.

"Goodness no," the white-haired gentleman answered, grinning at his petite partner. "I think this is our fifteenth, isn't it, my love? We're hooked on school!"

Harry and I got to know them that week as we tramped the woods in search of flora and fauna, panned for gold in the mountain streams, and giggled over our attempts at conversational Spanish. Our classmates and instructors got to know them, too, because they were as interested in people as they were in academia. They radiated a magnetic kind of enthusiasm—a zest for life.

When we learned that Maude and Otis were Christians, I was reminded of the root meaning of the word *enthusiasm*: God within. They are thoroughly enjoying themselves as they blaze a trail into their golden years for the younger members of their family to follow.

We can model faith.

Although our responsibilities diminish as the years go by, our losses do not. Little by little we are bound to lose many of the attributes that have kept us independent, self-assured, and physically attractive. We lose health, friends, and family members.

Our elderly neighbor, Arne, lost his leg after a long bout with bone disease. Not long after that, he lost his wife of fifty-three years to cancer. For a while the little house on the corner was quiet, and I missed his cheerful wave as I walked down the hill to our village. Then one day he was there again, tending his manicured garden, smiling and lifting a hand in greeting to passersby. Arne had lost many things, but he had not lost heart. You might say that he is blazing a trail through adversity for those of us who watch him. He is living out Paul's words:

> Therefore we do not lose heart. Though outwardly we are wasting away, yet inwardly we are being renewed day by day. For our light and momentary troubles are achieving for us an eternal glory that far outweighs them all. So we fix our eyes not on what is seen, but on what is unseen. For what is seen is temporary, but what is unseen is eternal (2 Cor. 4:16).

Our children will be watching us as we live out the years ahead of them. I pray that we can blaze a trail they will find worthy of following as we model flexibility, enthusiasm, and faith. My most fervent prayer is that they will "fix their eyes" not on us but on the "unseen" and choose to follow the One who leads us.

THE "GRAND" COMMISSION

Grandparenting is one of the commissions of our rear-guard station as older parents. Whether or not we are geographically or emotionally close to our grandchildren, we can be sure that our influence on their parents will spill over to impact their lives. Grandchildren, the inheritors of our family system, will benefit from its stability or suffer from its dysfunctional elements. We will affect our grandchildren indirectly, and we will have the ongoing opportunity to affect them directly.

My father, though not a demonstrative man, was a gifted letter writer. He used his gift to connect with his grandchildren, writing personal letters of encouragement or congratulations as the circumstances warranted. One of his last letters was directed to a newborn great-grandson and will be that child's link to his heritage as the years go by.

Since Connie's grandchildren live in a distant state, she goes without seeing them for years at a time, yet she keeps connected by sending cards for every occasion—Easter, Valentine's Day, graduations. Sometimes she sends her own creation, celebrating Groundhog Day or National Wildflower Week. Between times she talks to each of her grandchildren on the phone, keeping track of their current interests. Even though they don't see Grammy very often, Connie has a special and important place in her grandchildren's lives.

Harry and I delight in each of our sixteen grandchildren. We are free to love them "with no strings attached," to be more unconditionally loving than the duties of parenting had allowed us to be with our own. As each of our sixteen little ones came into the world, we marveled anew at the miracle of creation, seeing each grandchild's uniqueness with no temptation to compare one against the other. When one child took her first steps at nine months and another was still crawling at sixteen months, who cared? The young parents may have felt some competition among themselves, but we'd lived long enough to know how little these statistics count in the long run. The grandbabies brought Harry and me closer in a new way, too. His flesh and blood or mine, we could love them mutually and equally. They were God's compensation for the children we'd never had together.

In this reconnaissance period of our lives, when the major issues of parent-child separation have been confronted and at least partially resolved, we shift focus from what we have lost in relationship to what remains. We discover that we are not doomed to a life of dreary leftovers and crumbs of attention in our connections with our grown children. We can have a very significant—though more distant—place in their lives. We discover that the greatest love gift we can give them is the example of our own lives well-lived.

QUESTIONS FOR YOU

1. Which of your "midlife crises" has coincided with a crisis in the life of your adult child?

2. When have you been particularly sensitive (like the soft-shelled lobster) to changes in your adult child's life?

3. Can you find a "cause"—a reason for living—outside of your parental role?

4. What kind of changes are you seeing in your spiritual and marital relationship now that your children are grown?

5. In what ways can you continue to show your care and concern for your adult child?

6. In what ways can you be a trailblazer for your adult children?

• 7 •

Selective Service

Knowing When and How to Help

"No! No! I do it! Mommy go 'way!'"

You can probably remember hearing words like those almost as soon as your children could talk. They might have come from a small son as you coaxed him into his coveralls or washed the day's grime from his cherubic face. Chances are you backed off and let him dress or wash himself, however badly. According to the books you read, your toddler's bid for independence was a predictable and necessary stage of his development. Most of the time you were able to suppress your own pride (what would people think if you let him out to play in that outfit?) and overlook the inside-out shirt and the mismatched socks.

Like our toddlers, our adult children often push us away when we try to offer help or advice. Why is it that we see our little one's rebellion as a healthy expression of development, but when an adult child refuses help we feel rebuffed and rejected?

"I feel as if a door has been slammed in my face," said Liz, as the ladies of our Bible study group gathered for a fellowship luncheon. "When Jimmy was two and pushed me out of his room because he wanted to dress himself, the

• 113 •

consequences were minor. Who cared if his overalls were twisted or his shirt the wrong color? But when he's thirty-five and tells his father and me to stay out of his life, it's a different matter. We watch him heading for disaster and feel duty-bound to do everything in our power to stop him. What we see as loving concern, Jim calls interference. We have the wisdom of our own experience—some of it painful—to share and we can help in some practical ways, but he won't give us a chance."

Many parents feel duty-bound, as Liz expressed it, to correct what they see as errors in their children's lives. Other parents are successful in distancing themselves, emotionally if not literally, from their adult children and concentrating on their own affairs. But our God-given protective instinct to rescue dies hard, if at all.

Where and when to draw the line in helping is the dilemma for every conscientious parent. For how many years (and under what circumstances) should we exert our authority to protect our children? And how do we differentiate between serving our children's real needs and retarding their progress in self-sufficiency? Are they really serious when they tell us to stay out of their business? The confusion increases as our children mature and it remains after they are grown.

A GIVING PROFESSION

When we first became parents, there was no question about our positions of authority over our children or our areas of service to them. With a little help from our spouses, advice from a more experienced neighbor, and backup from Dr. Spock, we made all the decisions concerning our babies' physical and psychological welfare. We decided when to introduce baby cereal to the diet and when to switch from breast milk to formula. If there were protests, we wooed our small charges into cooperation with smiles and reassuring pats. We made decisions based on the needs and desires of our children, overruling their childish demands when necessary for their ultimate good. With our maternal nurturing instincts at their peak, we gave of ourselves on a twenty-four-hour-a-day basis, begrudging nothing, expecting nothing in return. Parenting is a giving profession.

We began as eager servants, not counting the cost. A few hours of lost sleep was a small price to pay for the indescribable joy we experienced as we cuddled our newborn infants.

Eventually, though, our precious charges rebelled at our authority, spit out their vitamins and threw their baby dishes on the floor, splattering strained sweet potatoes on the new kitchen wallpaper. From that moment on, there was tension and compromise between generations.

When a young mother's energy is depleted and her patience challenged by a sudden uprising, her selflessness begins to fade. This may be God's way of rescuing our children from a lifetime of overindulgence!

For our children, the journey from helpless infancy to competent adulthood was a long and complicated one. At every step of the way they fought for an independence that they were incapable of handling. They insisted on tying their shoelaces before they'd learned to make a bow and ran away with laces trailing, laughing until they tripped and fell. Then and not before could we get close enough to dry the tears and apply a Band-Aid to the scraped knee. Later, they resisted and resented our nagging about homework until they were humbled by pressing deadlines and threats of failing grades; then our offers to stay up and type the term papers were gratefully accepted.

We were confused and often angry. Our authority was rejected while our service was taken for granted. God had provided us with skills for both roles. It was our task to try to maintain an appropriate balance between the two elements, remembering that our primary role was to help our children grow up.

In the ideal situation, the final battles between parent and child were fought and resolved on the adolescent front. A truce was achieved, with concessions on both sides, and the older generation began its withdrawal to the rear guard—from active parenting to supportive parenthood. The process is gradual, and some of us have had a harder time than others in making a comfortable adjustment. The circumstances within our homes differ. We need to determine our own timetables for separation, knowing that separation is a prerequisite for a healthy adult relationship.

YES, BUT . . .

Parents who remain in the forefront of their adult children's lives usually have their reasons.

● We don't consider Bill a full-fledged adult, even though he is twenty-eight years old. He's been involved in drugs since he was a teenager, and everyone knows that keeps a person from maturing normally. His wife and the rest of the family have given up on him and he was literally without a roof over his head until we let him come home. How can his dad and I desert him now when he needs us so desperately?

A family friend's observation is that Bill only needs his parents when he runs out of buddies willing to support him and his habit. He moves back into the security of his parents' home and resumes the kind of life he had as an adolescent—working when it's convenient, sleeping until noon, watching TV or listening to music into the wee hours of the morning. His parents hold their breath, praying that this time he is off the drugs for good (naive in thinking he is off drugs at all), afraid to rock the boat and send him into the streets again.

● Dorothy has gotten herself into a financial and legal tangle that she can't get out of by herself. Of course it's not the first time. We promised ourselves last summer that we'd never get involved again, because she didn't seem to appreciate our help. She makes more money than we ever did, but nothing but the best is good enough for our Dot, so she buys whatever takes her fancy. Now the government is after her for back income tax. Maybe if we pull her out of the hole this time . . .

That was last year. Eight months later Dorothy is up to her elbows in debt again, and her parents are making a valiant effort to back off. Their efforts are aided by their own financial position and by family friction. Dorothy's brother is furious that his parents have drained their life savings to bail out his sister again.

● I feel totally responsible for the problems Eddie is having today. Because of my own problems, I was a terrible mother during the crucial years of his childhood. His father was never around, but that was my fault, too. Eddie missed out on the kind of love and support that would have helped him grow into a capable, responsible adult. If I can help find him a decent job or buy school clothes for the grandkids or send his wife a little spending money, well, I think I owe it to him.

Eddie is forty-two years old. It's very true that he had an unfortunate childhood, deprived of much of the emotional nurturing that every child deserves. But part of the maturing process for each of us is taking inventory of the assets and liabilities that we bring to adulthood, forgiving our parents for their contribution to our flaws and weaknesses (and, conversely, appreciating them for whatever part they played in the development of our strengths), and taking over responsibility for our present and future choices.

● Sheri's decision to divorce Paul is too important for us to stay out of. It's going to affect our grandchildren for the rest of their lives, and they have a right to our protection. She may resent our interference, but we can't stand quietly by while she destroys her family, not if we have any influence at all!

This one hits close to home, and I couldn't be more sympathetic. I have stood in this mother's shoes, broken-hearted and powerless to prevent the painful divorce that tore one of our young families apart. My own agony sent me running for counsel, looking for a way to force my wisdom onto these young people. My counselor advised me to stay out of my son's marital problems. I could be supportive of each of them as individuals, she said, but I must not become involved with the issues. At times I rebelled against her cool professional advice and *did* get involved in their battle, but I might as well have tried to enter a foreign war with a slingshot and a bag of marshmallows.

I went to God in prayer first, last, and intermittently, and in the end I clung to his promise in Romans 8:28 that he would somehow, someday, work all these hurtful things together for good. My son and daughter-in-law and each of their children had committed their lives to Christ in happier days, and that remembrance is like an analgesic to my pain. My children's lives are in his hands, not mine. I need to keep reminding myself of that.

My heart still occasionally questions the "hands-off" advice I received. Why, if that's God's judgment, didn't he remove my throbbing maternal urge to protect my child and his loved ones from the pain of divorce? Is God giving me a picture of his holy parenthood, I wonder? Or a taste, in human terms, of the sorrow he feels when his children use their free will to turn from his way? I don't know those answers. I can only share my own unfinished story and listen to the stories of others who long to save their adult children from the pain of life.

Every parent I interviewed had valid reasons for being involved in his or her adult child's life. Every experience, with minor alterations, could have been my own. I stand beside the bewildered mothers who don't know how to stifle their maternal inclination to rescue. Our God-given instincts make us feel obliged to respond to the perceived needs of our children. Our desire, if not our privilege, is to guide and direct our children safely past life's treacherous pitfalls.

In making decisions about when and how much to help our own adult children, we are bound to draw from the experience we've had with our parents.

DRAWING ON MEMORY

Looking back on my own years as an adult child, from the time I married and left home until my parents died several years ago, I see the many areas in my life where my parents' support made a crucial difference. They were not perfect parents, nor was I an easy daughter, but they played a supportive role in my life that no one else could have filled.

When World War II ended, I was nineteen and eager to get on with the happily-ever-after part of life. I took for granted my parents' willingness to provide a home for me and my young husband—a dental student within a few months of his degree. I had no idea of the personal sacrifice Mom and Dad were making as they took us into their home. I see now that they had little choice, given the postwar housing crunch, a first grandchild on the way, and a son-in-law who was not yet able to support a family.

For whatever reason, I had missed developing the kind of maturity I needed to begin a family of my own and was still clinging to my childhood family. I have wondered what would have happened if my parents had refused their help in those years. Perhaps the marriage that eventually crumbled would have ended sooner—or become stronger. Or maybe I would have been forced to grow up faster, to everyone's benefit. I know I would have been hurt and resentful toward my parents, and my relationship with them would have been changed forever.

I learned early to count on my parents' help in every crisis. Later, life taught its own hard lessons. My parents could rescue me in a financial emergency, but they could only stand by in love when my child died, my marriage ended in divorce, and the suspicious lump in my breast was diagnosed as malignant. I'm sure they grieved for me in my sorrows and prayed for me in my failures. Until my own children were grown, I had no way of understanding how deeply they felt my pain.

When I turned to my parents for comfort or compassion, they were generous in their response, loving me unconditionally, suppressing any urge to say, "We told you so." In that way they reflected God's love. Their willingness to meet whatever needs I brought to them never faltered, but their emotional energy faded with age.

There came a day when they began to lose interest in the details of my life—to maintain order in their own. Some of our conversations were vague and unfocused. I often came away from the telephone bewildered that some insignificant detail in their lives seemed to be taking precedence over my own crisis. My mother's cleaning woman had deserted her; *my* son had deserted the family and had been seen hanging out with the street people of Santa Barbara. My dad's new car was stalling on cold mornings; *my* hot water heater had flooded the house and there was no margin in the budget for a new one.

The psychological umbilical cord that connected me to my parents was a long time in dissolving. My acceptance of their humanness and my growing faith in a personal, omnipotent God effected the final work of separation.

Each of us had a unique experience with our own parents and brought that experience into parenting our own children. Most of us have appreciated and tried to emulate the positives and resisted our tendencies to perpetuate the negatives.

When one of our children needed financial help, I remembered the times I would have been in deep trouble without a "loan" from my parents. When another son's marriage was coming apart and I was frustrated in my futile attempts to intervene with advice, I needed to dredge up old memories of my own divorce. I remembered the resentment I felt toward my parents if they offered anything other than sympathy and understanding. Advice, however gentle and wise, sounded like criticism at that vulnerable time.

CHANGING TIMES

Times and traditions change with the generations. Our children are not carbon copies of us, nor are our relationships with them comparable to the relationships we had with our parents. We can use our own experience and personal memories as guidelines for judging our children's needs and expectations, but we will come closer to understanding what they want and don't want from us by listening to them and to their peers.

I talked to Naomi about her needs as a single adult. Did she welcome her parents' help in some situations?

"It kind of depends upon your definition of *help*," Naomi began. "Sometimes what my dad calls helping is what I call *controlling*. Like when he stormed into my boyfriend Gil's office and told him off. I'd made the mistake of telling Dad about an argument we'd had. In a moment of anger, Gil had hurt my feelings by saying I was spoiled and always had to have my own way. Maybe I was looking for sympathy or reassurance from Daddy, but I sure didn't expect him to confront Gil about it. I think Dad saw Gil's attitude as a personal insult to him as a parent, so he was really defending his pride rather than me. I don't think he'd intentionally break up my relationship with Gil, but I know he's been jealous of the time I've spent with him. Maybe he sees himself in some kind of competition with my friends—especially men."

Naomi's father would probably be surprised and hurt by his daughter's assessment of his motives. He feels righteously angry with Gil for hurting Naomi and probably thinks she could do better.

I asked Naomi what she really wanted from her dad when she confided in him about her argument with Gil. Her answer was revealing:

"I guess I was looking for the same kind of support I might find from a good friend. Come to think of it, I'd already told Nora, my best friend, about what Gil had said about my being spoiled and I got the feeling from *her* response that she might agree with him! Nora's childhood was what you could call underprivileged—very different from mine—and I wouldn't blame her for being envious of the love and security I had growing up. She probably thinks of that kind of nurturing as 'spoiling.' Maybe I feel a little guilty about it, myself. So, to answer your question, I probably wanted Daddy to reassure me that I wasn't spoiled. Mostly, I think, I just wanted him to listen and love me. But he always has to barge in and *do* something to fix things!"

I suggested to my young friend that she do what I would want my own daughter or son to do: tell her father how she felt. I helped her to understand that our protective-parent instincts are hard to rechannel. We need feedback and direction from our children as we make the transition from active parenting to supportive parenthood, even if it means risking hurt feelings. Most of us have good intentions. We only want to smooth some of life's bumps for our adult children.

LISTENING AND LOVING

Naomi expressed the greatest desire of each of us when she said, "I just wanted him to listen and love me." All of us need a safe place to pour out feelings without danger of being judged. Naomi counted on her father to know her as well as anyone could. She expected him to understand her need for a shoulder to cry on, and yet, if she'd looked back, she would have realized that her father had always demonstrated his love with action. He'd been the kind of father who had leaped to his daughter's side in every neighborhood confrontation, and he hadn't been able to break the habit.

Parents have a difficult time taking an objective view of anything concerning their children. Emotion always intrudes upon reason. We sometimes listen poorly as we mentally devise plans of solution and rehearse our own heroic strategies for rescue. Like Naomi's father, most parents have difficulty recognizing their inclination to maneuver and manipulate in the name of love. We all do it, for a variety of reasons:

1. We've watched our children grow up making one mistake after another, and we've bailed them out when we could. We don't trust them to make decisions (or defend themselves) without our help.

2. We've built our lives around our parenting roles and we don't know who we are outside of that role. We may fear for our own reputations, thinking that if we're not seen as good parents, we're seen as failures at life.

3. We're reliving our own dreams and making up for lost opportunities through our adult children.

4. We are afraid to lose relationship with our child. We think that to retire from involvement in the many facets of our adult child's life is to lose our connection with him or her.

5. We love our adult children and want to spare them pain by steering them around the hazards that may have created problems in our own lives.

6. We forget that our children are only on loan to us, that ultimately they belong to their heavenly Father who may want us to back off and let him work in their lives.

WHEN HELP IS A HINDRANCE

Sometimes the withdrawal of inappropriate help is the best service of all to our children. Parents who deal with drug-abusing children often learn this the hard way.

Shawn, whose story I told in *Understanding Alcoholism*,[1] is an example of a young adult who was helped in his recovery from drug abuse by his parents' eventual *refusal* to help. Shawn said, "My mom fit the picture of the Enabler to a T. I learned to play upon her sympathy until she was taking on the whole bag of responsibility for my drinking and using drugs. I couldn't con my dad so easily, and he and my mom almost broke up over how they should handle me. If she hadn't gone to Al-Anon and found out how to 'let go with love,' as she puts it, I might never have had to face myself and get into recovery."

Al-Anon, a fellowship of relatives and friends of alcoholics and abusers of other drugs, teaches the principle of loving detachment. Detachment from a son or daughter who is suffering from an addictive disease may seem heartless, but it is necessary for the health and sanity of those who are dealing with an addicted loved one and has proven to increase the chances for his recovery. Since drug abuse is an all too frequent factor in the conflicts between parents and their adult children, the Al-Anon philosophy deserves some review here.

Al-Anon is a spiritual, nonsectarian program that offers invaluable help to family members and friends of alcoholics and those addicted to other substances. Al-Anon believes that addiction is a family illness, contagious in its effects on every member of the addict's family. Because of the nation's escalating drug problem, many participants in the Al-Anon program are parents of young adults with problems of addiction. The typical parent comes to the fellowship of Al-Anon after trying everything in his or her power to stop his child from drinking or using. He has wept and pleaded and bribed and scolded to no avail, and he has finally become desperate enough to turn for help to others who are learning to cope with similar circumstances. Soldiers in battle call for reinforcements.

Al-Anon members help one another practice the principle of detachment. They "let go with love," as Shawn said, and focus on their own attitudes, finding healing for themselves in the final realization that they are not responsible for their loved one's addiction. They didn't cause it, they can't control it, and they can't cure it. They begin to find some peace and order in their lives as they learn

- not to suffer because of the actions or reactions of other people;
- not to allow themselves to be used or abused in the interest of another's recovery;
- not to do for others what they should do for themselves;
- not to manipulate situations so others will eat, go to bed, get up, pay bills, etc.;
- not to cover up for another's mistakes or misdeeds;
- not to create a crisis;
- not to prevent a crisis if it is in the natural course of events.[2]

This is hard, hard, hard! If addiction is an illness and our children are sick, shouldn't we be bending over backward to help them get well? Yes, of course, say those who have gone before, but this practice of detachment is the best help you can give your adult child.

Detachment doesn't mean desertion. Sometimes teens can be successfully forced into treatment for addiction, and sometimes the technique of intervention can lead to an adult's recovery, but those steps are better taken with emotional detachment. If they are to be effective, our actions and attitudes need to come from a position of strength, so shifting our focus from our addicted loved one to our own healing must come first.

The principle of detachment could be successfully applied to many parent/adult-child issues other than drug dependence.

For instance, Steve is a young man who simply refuses to grow up. In the five years since his graduation from high school, he's been unable to make decisions about his future. Several times Steve has begun a course at the local college only to drop out before the semester ends. If he finds a job—usually with the help of a family member—he soon becomes bored and quits. Steve's parents are understandably grateful that their son hasn't gotten involved with the drug crowd or run afoul of the law. "He'll find himself one of these days," his mother says. "In the meantime, we can help by letting him live at home and use one of our cars." Like other parents in similar circumstances, they may come to realize that their help is *not* help if it fails to bring about change in their son's immature behavior.

DOLLAR DILEMMAS

One of the most sensitive areas of relationship between parent and adult child is that of lending, borrowing, or giving money. Most of our young adults do not build up a substantial savings account or a financial cushion for emergencies during the first years of their independence. During that time their lives are particularly vulnerable to invasion by illness, accident, or unemployment. When children are in trouble due to circumstances beyond their control, loving parents can hardly turn their backs.

After their son lost his job, one family volunteered to pay his rent until he got on his feet again. Friends whose daughter is a single mother struggling to make ends meet visit her often to bring groceries, take the children for haircuts and new shoes, and do maintenance chores around her deteriorating home. Their support will keep her going until her children are in school and she can find full-time employment.

In many cases the need is not so clear-cut, and parents vacillate between the urge to help and the responsibility they feel for letting go. You see a daughter driving an old car with balding tires. Should you offer to buy new tires, knowing she and her husband are in a financial bind, or will your son-in-law resent the interference? If you leave the problem in their camp, where you suspect it belongs, do you risk allowing an accident where someone could be badly injured?

Many young married couples have no hope of buying a home of their own without a little help from his or her parents. Should the parents forego a long-awaited trip to Europe in order to provide the necessary down payment for a son or daughter's dream home? There are no absolute guidelines for these decisions. If families have developed open and honest communication between generations, they can confront the problem together. If parents don't have the resources to give financial aid, they can suggest options or direct the young people to someone who can give financial advice.

Many parents sacrifice their personal needs to give their children financial assistance. Some give grudgingly, others are generous to a fault. Some adult children receive gifts or loans from their parents with sincere gratitude; others take it for granted or feel it is their due. In most cases, money gifts from parents to children work better than loans. Gifts should have no subtle strings attached to keep the recipient in grateful bondage to the giver.

Whatever the circumstances and reactions of the individuals involved, when financial help is given or accepted between parent and adult child, the relationship is altered forever. Often, relationships between parents and other members of the family are changed as well, subtly or dramatically.

One father said, "Sometimes one of the kids will put me on the spot by asking for help I'm unable to give, and other times I feel hampered in giving help to one kid because another will hear about it and resent it. It's really a touchy area in our family."

Pat and Lloyd chose to loan money to their son Aaron and not to his brother Keith, a decision that created dissension within the entire family. Although a cease-fire was finally acheived, the resentment is likely to come up again sometime in the future, unless Pat and Lloyd are especially sensitive to the competitive feeling between the brothers. Their story has endless variations. Some families have been permanently broken in disputes involving loans or gifts of money (or other valuables) from parent to adult child.

Family conflict stirred up by financial issues can persist for a lifetime, well beyond the reading of the parents' last will and testament. Our final bequests may be met with displeasure or shock or resentment bitter enough to bring sibling rivalry to its final destructive head and separate the children we have loved. We can only pray for wisdom in preventing such an eventuality, being aware that we may be strengthening or weakening ties as we make "giving" decisions now.

Most of us will be forced at some time or another to make decisions about helping our children financially. They will come to us for assistance, or we will discover their need. In meeting the need or refusing the request, we will sometimes make mistakes. We may be put in a position where any choice we make will offend someone. We may alienate our children even as we give, because we will imply, or they will suspect, "strings" attached to our generosity.

My parents managed to keep things amazingly even between my brother and me; we have never had a conflict over material things. Because Harry and I have never succeeded in keeping things even among our nine, we can anticipate occasional ruffled feelings. Sometimes a decision that seems wise to us is viewed as foolish by one or more of our adult children. Sometimes the major conflict is between Harry and me, when we can't agree on how best to help one of our flock.

Emotions rise and tempers flare where money issues become entangled with our relationships. Paul had undoubtedly seen "ruin and destruction" of precious family relationships when he warned, "For the love of money is a root of all kinds of evil" (1 Tim 6:10). He does not tell us here to scorn money itself, only the love of it.

The borrowing or lending of money is a touchy area in most families. Whether or not to help adult children financially and how to do so are issues that require much consideration and prayer.

TWO-SIDED ISSUES

I was part of a group of women of varying ages that met for lunch one day recently. The table conversation helped me understand some of the problems both generations experience in giving or receiving help.

"I've spent the last thirty years raising children," said Georgia. "My daughters tell me it's time for me to quit mothering and find something else to think about, but it's going to take me a while to develop some other interests. Of course, I'm always welcome when they need me to baby-sit or pick someone up at school or help out in other ways, but they don't want my advice anymore and they've stopped sharing anything personal with me. They say they want me to stop mothering, but they expect me to help them with *their* mothering on demand."

Georgia has a valid complaint, but there's probably another side to her story. Her daughters may feel something like Shelley, a younger member of our group, who said, "One reason I want to stay close to my folks is so my kids will have a relationship with their grandparents that I never had. When I ask Mom and Dad to take the boys while Dave and I go on vacation, my motive is partly selfish, because I don't worry about them nearly so much when they're with their grandparents, but it's partly because I think both generations are missing out if they don't have the opportunity to spend time together."

"That's true," said silver-haired Karen. "We can't get to know our grandchildren from a distance. I know I'm a lot closer to the grandchildren I helped take care of when they were babies than the ones that came along later, when I was involved with my own series of illnesses. My daughter was only twenty when Alyssa, our first grandchild, was born, and she really needed my support. But then I was only forty myself and had a lot more energy than I do now! You young moms may not realize that some days taking on a two-year-old seems like an overwhelming task!"

Heads nodded in assent as Phyllis spoke, a hint of sadness in her tone. "Joe and I love our grandchildren dearly, and we're willing to help our daughters out once in a while by keeping the kids, but it seems like that's the only time we hear from them—when they want us to baby-sit."

"I'm afraid my mother feels like that at times," Shelley said. "The last time I called her was to ask if the boys could stay with them over the Fourth of July holiday. Dave wants me to go to San Francisco with him, and we really need some time together. The boys are too old for a babysitter, but we sure can't leave them alone at fifteen and seventeen! I hesitated to call Mom, because I hadn't talked to her for a couple of weeks. She probably feels just like Phyllis—that the only time she hears from me is when I want something. It's just that our lives are so chaotic lately. I just hope she understands."

We older parents should have an easier time understanding the needs of our adult children than they have understanding our needs. I was once a thirty-five-year-old mom; my daughter has never been a sixty-year-old grandma. If she is like I was, she may not be able to conceive of my having an agenda of my own that I consider important!

Although I understand many of my daughter's problems, I also realize that her situation is different than mine was twenty-five years ago. My frustrations often came from being housebound with small children; hers come from juggling a family and a career. I wanted to break out of my four walls and spend an afternoon window-shopping or talking to adults; my daughter yearns to stay home for a while and just be a mom.

Twenty-nine-year-old Crystal turned to Georgia. "Your saying your daughters don't share personal things with you anymore makes me wonder if my mom feels the same way. I've given up telling her very much of anything. Every time I try to talk to my mom about some crisis I'm going through or even when I just express my feelings about something, she goes into this long tirade about how sensitive I was as a little girl and how I mustn't take myself so seriously and how my diet is probably affecting my nerves! She says she doesn't mean to be critical and that she's just trying to help, but her kind of help I can do without. She thinks if I can't see a situation from her point of view, I'm not being realistic. We're so different, Mom and I. I guess we'll never have a meeting of the minds, so the things we can talk about are really limited. I wish she'd just take me as I am."

I have a theory. Could it be that we parents have an ongoing (albeit subconscious) desire to mold our children into people more like us, with personalities we can understand, just so we can have a closer relationship with them?

DIVIDED LOYALTIES

Peggy finds herself in an awkward position between her two adult children and her husband, Karl. "Believe me," she says, "I'm more than willing to give up my responsibility for Andy's and April's lives. At twenty-nine and thirty-two, they can take charge of their own decisions. I don't want either the credit or the blame for what they do! I never was very good at the authority role, anyway, so I mostly left that up to Karl. What's confusing me now is where to draw the line in *helping*.

"For instance, Brent, April's husband, has decided to go back to school and get his MBA, so April plans to work part-time to supplement their income. Fine. No one asked my opinion, but I think it's great. What they *did* ask for was my help in watching Kerry after school. She's eight, so she's easy to have around, but Karl's already pouting about my not being available to do things. We didn't change our vacation plans—April has a friend who will fill in for two weeks—but Karl likes to go places on the spur of the moment. He's worried, too. about school vacations and that this might escalate into a full-time responsibility. I've been in a quandary about it, feeling torn between my husband and my daughter."

Peggy's problem set us to talking about the conflict of loyalties that so often arises when we try to please both our husbands and our children. Two of us had blended families and probably felt some extra tugs when our loyalties were divided between our children and their stepfathers, but all of us could identify with Peggy's situation.

Anna, whose husband was newly retired, spoke. "I think, if it comes to a draw, our husbands' needs should take precedence over our adult children. Oh, I suppose there are exceptions, in cases of illness or something, but April's situation is hardly an emergency. Maybe you could arrive at some sort of compromise where you could pick and choose when to care for Kerry, and April could work just when Kerry is in school. I know my niece is sharing an office job, so she can be home when the children are out of school. There are other solutions to their problem."

Fifty-year-old Lois brought up another common situation. "Peggy is torn between her husband's needs and her daughter's, but our conflict is between our grown children and our elderly parents. We're in what they call the 'sandwich generation.' So many times they both need our attention, and we're not sure who comes first or who's more helpless. We feel like we're parenting in both directions!"

"I hear that same thing from my folks about my grandma," someone said. "And sometimes I find myself getting jealous of the time Mom and Dad have to spend with Grandma when I'd like them to pay more attention to my family. It seems all of us are torn in so many ways! It really is hard to understand where the other person is coming from when you're all tied up with your own problems."

BY TRIAL AND ERROR

I came away from our group discussion with the distinct impression that each woman who spoke placed high value upon her intergenerational relationships. We mothers of grown children like the idea that we are still needed in some areas of their lives. But then we sometimes feel taken for granted and often would like to help with advice that's unheeded or unwelcome. Both generations yearn for understanding and seek ways to maintain or strengthen ties, but the older generation appears to have a harder time finding where we fit in our children's lives.

By trial and error most of us eventually find where our help is welcome in our adult children's lives and where we are intruding upon their privacy. We must be willing to find new areas of service and new ground for communication or we will risk losing the close bond that will bless and enrich the lives of both generations.

It's hard to stand aside when your children are in need and you have the ability to help them. You may be intruding when you think you are helping; you may be "enabling" when you intend to be supporting. You will have to decide upon your own place of service.

As you face difficult decisions in helping your children, be assured that God loves them more than you ever could. He cares about what is happening to them at this very moment. He sees into their hearts and is familiar with every detail of their lives. He waits for and hears your prayers for their protection and happiness. God has a wonderful plan for the lives of each of your children and he will nudge them in that direction.

We can serve our children best by praying that they will find his gentle nudging irresistible.

QUESTIONS FOR YOU

1. When, if ever, have you felt confused about how far to go or where to draw the line in helping your adult child?

2. Have you experienced resentment from other family members when you chose to help an adult child? How have you handled the dissension?

3. Do you feel that you owe one of your adult children a little extra help? For what reason?

4. Under what circumstances do you feel parents should unhesitatingly help their adult children?

5. Under what circumstances do you think parents should *not* help their adult children?

6. In what ways do you tend to follow your parents' example in helping your adult children?

7. What are your feelings about giving money or substantial material gifts to your adult children?

8. Do you ever have a conflict of loyalties between the needs of your adult children and your husband? Between your adult children and your own parents? Between one adult child and another?

9. Can you identify specific areas in which you can be of service to your children today?

· 8 ·

Recalled to Active Duty
When Kids Come Home Again

Thirtysome years ago the young moms of Cypress Way gathered around my kitchen table, sipping coffee and overseeing our collective children. Two infants shared a playpen in the corner of the dining room, three little boys played underfoot, making block tunnels for their cars, and a group of five- and six-year-olds tumbled on the lawn outside.

Betty, an older neighbor, stood in the doorway smiling at us. "Enjoy it while you can," she said. "These years will speed by. Before you know it they'll be grown and gone like mine."

We knew that. These little ones, who in the fifties absorbed ninety percent of our time and energy, would grow up to establish homes and families of their own. That was the one predictable element of our foggy futures. We would be gray-haired grandmas, living out our sunset years in empty nests. All of that was a millennium away, and we were too busy to think about it much then, but we lived with that reasonable expectation.

Life is not necessarily reasonable. One of those little boys has never left home, and one of the young mothers died before her children grew up. But for the rest of us, the empty-nest years arrived as scheduled. Our children may have moved in and out a few times in the beginning of their adult years, but at some point we found ourselves converting the kids' bedrooms into offices and sewing rooms. We mentally prepared ourselves for this natural course of events. We adjusted our lifestyles and filled the empty places with new interests.

What most of us weren't prepared for was the refilling of the nest and the problems involved when our once-independent children came home again. One journalist called it the boomerang syndrome—a phenomenon that's happening more and more often. Our kids are trying to maintain their independence in a society where divorce is prevalent, unemployment is rampant, and affordable housing is at an all-time low. They've not had time to build a cushion of security against an unforeseen emergency. They're stretched to the limit getting into a first house or apartment, and one setback can wipe them out.

Young people who have stand-by parents, ready and willing to help their children through adversity, are fortunate. Some of these parents find the most effective way of helping is to reopen their doors and welcome their adult children home again. "It's only temporary," a parent says. And "Just until they can resolve their problems," says another. But "just until" sometimes stretches beyond endurance, and problems are apt to multiply—especially on the side of the older generation.

I ran into Virginia at Food-for-Less. She looked frazzled.

"What's the occasion?" I asked, eyeing her cart overflowing with groceries. "Family reunion?"

"No," she sighed, "Just the weekly shopping. Bert and I aren't alone anymore, you know. Our son, Lance, lost his job at the plant and they couldn't make the rent on Linda's salary alone, so they're staying with us for a while. That crazy Lance broke his arm trying to move their freezer by himself, and Linda just found out she's pregnant!

"We thought it would be a temporary thing," Virginia continued, "but it's dragging on. Lance found a job, finally, but they haven't been able to get ahead enough to move into their own place. So much for our empty nest! I hate to complain. We love Lance and Linda both, but we were ready to kick back and relax a little. I wasn't ready for this."

AMBIVALENT FEELINGS

Virginia expressed how thousands of us feel when, for one reason or another, our adult children return to the nest. We're concerned for our children and whatever crisis has brought them home again. We want to help. We love being needed, especially if we felt rejected during the first separation or if we've had twinges of jealousy over their new friends, engrossing careers, or inlaws. Parents are naturally programmed to be needed.

So our negative reactions are confusing. When we feel disappointment over our own thwarted empty-nest plans, we judge ourselves selfish. We feel guilty and wonder at our lack of parental enthusiasm. Some of us are experiencing a personal or marital crisis that drains us of the emotional energy necessary to take on the parenting role again. Our sons and daughters may need our financial support at the very time we are trimming expenses in preparation for retirement. If they bring *their* children, we may also find ourselves exhausted by the constant noise and confusion.

Virginia's statement that she "wasn't ready for this" points out the first problem our generation has with adult children who move home again. We aren't ready. Our culture has prepared us for separation. Our expectations of life beyond the emptying of the nest didn't include its refilling. We've weathered the psychological trauma of releasing our young adults to their chosen journeys. We've plugged the holes in our lives with careers or classes or hobbies that have been on hold, we've moved out the old bunk beds and set up the new computer, and we're saving any extra cash for that long-awaited trip to Europe.

We are happy and comfortable within our empty nests. This may come as a surprise to our adult children, who have been busy piloting their own ship of independence and see us as freeze-framed in our old places on shore. When the storms come up and the seas get too rough to navigate, who can blame them for turning back to a safe harbor? We keep our dismay to ourselves, reluctant to turn our children away when they're in need, guilty if we even entertain the thought.

Guilty. That word kept coming up in my conversations with parents (especially mothers) whose adult children had moved home again. Virginia felt guilty about complaining. Mothers were supposed to discount their own needs when their children were in trouble, weren't they? And so she had, willingly. But she was tired and missed having the house to herself. At home, she swallowed her objections and refilled her prescription for tranquilizers.

MISGUIDED MARTYRDOM

Virginia was determined to make the best of a hard situation. She owed Lance that much, she thought. And poor Linda, having to go to work feeling queasy every morning. Virginia's heart was right, but her suppressed feelings forced her into a role of silent martyrdom. Before long the formerly relaxed atmosphere in their home bristled with tension.

The most effective antidotes for this kind of guilt-propelled martyrdom—suffering in silence rather than expressing valid needs—are communication and compromise.

Each adult involved in the reorganized family has the right and the responsibility to speak out. We need to be open to listen to the frustrations of the younger generation as they are forced into dependency again. On the other hand, they need to listen to us as well. Our children can't be expected to know our frustrations unless we express them. Their memories have preserved us in the "nurturing parent" mode. Their earlier years taught them to take us for granted, and they can hardly conceive of us retiring from active parenting by *choice*.

Jeanne and Tom decided to be straightforward with their daughter Lori when she asked to come home again.

"To be honest, I was tempted to bar the door," Tom said. "Our youngest had just gotten married, and Jeanne and I were in the process of rearranging our lives when Lori turned up on our doorstep."

"Tom still had a few years before retirement," Jeanne said, "so I'd made the big decision to go back to school and get my degree. What a shock when I came home on my first day of classes to find Lori and four-year-old Zachary sitting on our patio surrounded by their luggage!

"My first reaction, like Tom's, was to blow up. We had begged and pleaded with Lori not to marry Greg, but she wouldn't listen, and now here she was home again. I held my tongue, because Lori didn't need to hear me say 'I told you so' at that point. She'd made a mistake, but I'd made a few myself over the years. We've always told our girls that we can trust the Lord for strength in every circumstance, and I figured this was one of those circumstances. Lori needed his strength and so did we."

"Jeanne convinced me we could work it out," Tom said. "I insisted that she follow through with school, and I didn't want her worn out with extra work, so I made it clear to Lori that our needs would have equal priority with hers. For instance, I wasn't about to give up my new den, so we put an extra bed in Lori's room for Zach. Naturally the little guy spreads out and we're tripping over toys in the hallway, but I guess we can put up with that for the time being. I expected to have to compromise."

"It hasn't been such a bad deal for me," Jeanne said. "For now, Lori's doing the housework and cooking, so I just dress and go in the morning. We've forfeited our quiet evenings, but I've learned to study at the library. Zach will start preschool in September and then Lori can look for a job and think about getting out on her own.

"Tom and I have done a lot of praying for patience, and God has shown us some real blessings in our situation. We're getting closer to our grandson than we could have under any other circumstances, and Lori and I are developing a special friendship. She left home as a young rebel, and it took a toll on our relationship. Now we're relating as two adult women and finding that we each have strengths to share. Because we respect each other as adults, it's working. It hasn't been easy, but we've come a long way in the last few months."

Honest communication and willingness to compromise made the difference in this family merger.

THE GENERATION GAP

We've had little or no modeling for living in a multi-generational household. In the nineteenth century it was common for three or even four generations to live together in reasonable harmony. Many hands made lighter work, both in the fields and in running the household. Family members worked together toward mutual goals, and the authority of the older generation was respected.

Traditions change. We've come to a time in history when we believe in and encourage independence—even distance—between nuclear families. When circumstances unite two generations into one household, we hardly know how to act. If parents try to take up where they left off, treating their grown children like adolescents, they find they've lost their authority.

"I think this is the hardest part of having my daughter back home again," said an old friend. "We have absolutely no say in what she does. Megan's lifestyle drives Ed and me wild sometimes. Her permissiveness with her children, the way she spends money she should be saving for a new start, and her bizarre social life are so foreign to us. When she's living right under our noses, we can't keep quiet. And yet she says it's none of our business!

"When I was Megan's age, I respected Mother and Dad's opinions. Of course, I wasn't living under their roof, so there were some things I chose not to share with them—like the time Ed and I spent our last twenty-five dollars on tickets to a concert and had to eat egg sandwiches for a week. That was a learning experience we kept to ourselves!

"It's natural for young people to make some mistakes in judgment and some poor choices, but I think it's natural for parents who see it happening to react. I don't want to know everything Megan is doing, and I wouldn't if she were in her own place. The way things are, I can't help letting her know when I disapprove of her habits. But it doesn't change anything—just puts another brick in the wall between us."

Adult children who have been independent for a period of time have established their own lifestyles. They may keep late hours, leave beds unmade and dishes in the sink, or associate with unconventional people. When they move home again, bringing their lifestyles with them, conflict is inevitable. Parents who once could lay down the law ("If you don't clean up your room, you can't use the car tonight!") are unsure of their place of authority over their live-in adult child. The training instinct dies hard as parents search for some middle ground between parenting an adolescent and hosting a weekend guest.

When returning adults bring spouses and/or children, the problems are compounded. Sons- and daughters-in-law may be handled with care, but where grandchildren are involved, grandparents usually feel justified in offering advice or expressing disapproval. The advice may be good and the disapproval warranted, but young parents are sensitive in this area and are apt to respond with resentment. A good rule of thumb here is for grandparents to stay out of child-raising issues unless they see abuse or neglect.

Child-*controlling* is another matter. Grandparents have a

right to protect their property. Statements like "Thank you for being careful of Grandma's new couch" shouldn't offend anyone.

Financial friction is also common between cohabiting generations. Parents who are paying higher utility and grocery bills are understandably disturbed when they see their adult children spending money frivolously. Comments from parents indicate that the generation gap may be at its widest in this area.

- "When I saw firsthand how my son-in-law spent every extra dime on fancy stereo equipment, I wasn't surprised they'd gotten in the bind they were in before they moved in with us."
- "These kids have to have everything they want, whether they can afford it or not. I couldn't believe the mess Jason got himself into with three credit cards and an ATM!"
- "We're careful to make our long-distance calls on weekends when the rates are low, but our daughter thinks nothing of talking to her boyfriend in San Francisco for half an hour at any time of day."

Parents should expect their live-in children to contribute to the household expenses as they are able. Otherwise they are encouraging irresponsibility—and adding to their own frustrations.

Parents who back away from conflict issues are apt to whisper their frustrations behind closed doors or share them with a friend rather than confront the culprits. But open conflict is often healthier than cold war. If communication of feelings fails to lead to understanding and cooperation from the younger generation, parents have a right to discontinue their hospitality.

HARD DECISIONS

I was moved by author Helen Hosier's account of her own experience. Her son, Barry, and daughter-in-law, Cheryl, lived with the nightmare of Cheryl's schizophrenia. Several times the young family needed the kind of help that Helen and her husband could give only by taking them into their home. It must have been incredibly difficult.

> There was never any question in our minds about what we had to do. It wasn't easy and it usually isn't, as most parents will admit. But I simply can't get away from the implications of a seldom-discussed proverb.[1]

Hosier points to Proverbs 3:27: "Do not withhold good from those who deserve it, when it is in your power to act." That verse validated the decision she and her husband made to welcome their son and his family into their home.

This proverb does not say to me that we must *always* open our doors to an adult child in trouble. It is not always within a parent's power to act, nor is it always good for the young person to be rescued from adversity.

Some caring parents are unable to help their children out of a crisis by opening their homes. They have neither the room, the energy, nor the financial ability to support another family. Others may find that in giving shelter to an adult child, they are endangering their own stability.

Ruth feels she placed her marriage in jeopardy when she took her twenty-eight-year-old daughter, Kris, and Kris's two children into her home.

"I should have known," Ruth said. "My husband, Ted, is Kris's stepfather. He's fond of Kris, but he'd never been around small children, and I knew how rambunctious two little boys could be. I got used to the noise and confusion, but Ted was so uptight all the time that Kris and I were walking on eggshells. Although I enjoyed having Kris around, I was crabbing at the boys all the time, and my relationship with Ted went downhill until something had to give. After a lot of soul-searching, I decided my marriage had to come first. Fortunately, Ted was more than willing to pay for Kris to get into an apartment. I don't know what we would have done otherwise. I couldn't have put her out into the street."

Ruth and Ted moved their daughter out of their home for the sake of their own declining relationship. Other parents have had to turn an adult child away in the best interest of that child.

In an earlier chapter, we discussed the "enabling" parents who encourage and perpetuate their children's dependent behavior by continually rescuing them from the consequences of that behavior. Sometimes, as in the case of a young adult addicted to drugs, allowing an adult child to return home is enabling rather than helping. The better decision, hard as it is, may be to say no to an adult child who wants to move home.

A VIEW FROM THE OTHER SIDE

As I listened to parents who were grappling with problems of boomerang children, I couldn't help but remember the post-war years when my husband and I had put my own parents in the same position. It was a revelation to me to see through the eyes of today's older parents what it must have been like for Mother and Dad to have us living with them. We settled into my old bedroom and redecorated my brother's room in ruffles and pastels for our expected child. My mother quietly tolerated my sewing projects cluttering her formal living room. My dad never said a word when he came home from work to find his favorite chair occupied by his new son-in-law.

I cringe to remember these things. I had thought then that we and other young married couples of that time were the only ones suffering the consequences of the housing crunch! Along with my delayed understanding of the problems my parents faced, I have rekindled memories that help me sympathize with the young people caught in today's boomerang trap.

I identified with Coralee when she said, "My parents were generous to take us in, but we'd rather not be here. When my mother treats me like a fifteen-year-old, I find myself behaving like one. I think we've lost enough without losing our dignity, too."

The loss of dignity is a key issue among the young people I interviewed. Their autonomy, the prize for which they've battled since their teens, is threatened. Their self-confidence was shattered by whatever failure brought them home again, and being treated like children further deflates their self-esteem. Unless they can make a real contribution to the household—and sometimes a contribution is only forthcoming on demand—they are apt to feel like charity cases.

Stacy, the daughter of a friend, shared her experience. "It's easy to feel like excess baggage unless you find something constructive to do," she said. "When Jeff and I moved home, we asked my dad if we could refinish the basement—something my folks had been planning to do for years. Jeff is a skilled carpenter and Daddy really doesn't like that sort of thing. I enjoy sewing, so I made some slipcovers for the old furniture. It gave us a place to be after work and on weekends, and we felt like we were paying for our keep a little. It's hard to take charity, even from your family."

When Lance and Linda finally moved to their own place again, Linda confided: "It was awful being dependent on Lance's parents for our bed and board. I didn't know Bert and Virginia well, so it was hard to know how to behave. I tried to help, but I had all-day "morning sickness," and I just wanted to collapse when I came home from work. And naturally Lance was hampered with his arm in a cast.

"We didn't want to make extra work, but of course we did. And when I volunteered to vacuum or do the laundry, I was never sure whether I was helping or intruding.

"Lance and I would have been happy to go out in the

evening and do the grocery shopping. We needed some time alone after work, and that would have given the folks a little space, too. But whenever we'd suggest doing anything, Virginia would say, 'Oh, that's okay,' and do it herself. I figured it was up to Lance to know what his mother really wanted."

Looking back, Lori was grateful for the ground rules Jeanne and Tom laid out as a condition for her returning home to live. "If they'd let me, I would have just crawled into a hole and felt sorry for myself," she said. "But Dad let me know they had plans of their own and I was going to have to carry my own weight. Keeping busy was healthy for me, and taking care of the household gave me a sense of accomplishment."

In this family, former parent-child roles gave way to a peer relationship where mutual dependency led to mutual respect.

SKIRMISHES

Besides being open and honest about frustrations and expectations from the beginning, both generations need to make an effort to maintain the peace of the shared household.

Two families living under one roof are bound to have occasional friction. If differences aren't resolved as they arise, a minor skirmish can escalate into an all-out battle or deteriorate into permanent cold war. That's what happened with Lisa and her mother-in-law.

"It all started with a minor disagreement about disposable diapers," said Lisa. "I said I thought everyone should go back to cloth diapers for the sake of ecology and economy, and Barb insisted our water shortage was more crucial than the mounting garbage. She threw in some remarks about my 'radical generation' and put me on the defensive. It was all very silly, but it hurt our relationship. Al and his dad got caught in the middle, and things haven't been right between us since. The longer it goes, the harder it is to try to make peace."

The consequences of Lisa's verbal battle with her mother-in-law remained long after the words themselves were forgotten.

"I should have swallowed my pride and apologized before it went any further," Lisa said. "Now we're all nursing grudges, and it's hard to break the ice."

A NEW CHALLENGE

The shape of the American family is continually changing. Empty nests are beginning to fill again as young adults lose their independence to a job lay-off, an uninsured accident, or a broken marriage. For the first time in recent history, we see many older parents securely settled in spacious, mortgage-free homes while their adult children work overtime to pay for inadequate housing. As this situation continues, we will be challenged with an increase in intergenerational living and its accompanying problems.

Family relationships are fragile and precious. The relationship between parent and adult child is easily damaged in situations of mutual stress, and mutual stress is a given when adult children return home. On the other hand, wonderful new relationships can develop as parents and children learn to communicate, cooperate, and respect one another as peers and valuable friends.

If you've been recalled to active duty and are faced with the challenge of living with your adult children, take heart. It can be a positive experience.

Here are some suggestions compiled from parents who have been there:
- Pray for patience, guidance, and a sense of humor.
- Set a time limit on your hospitality. It can always be renegotiated.

- Be honest at the beginning about your misgivings and your expectations.
- Lay out some ground rules and delegate responsibilities.
- Expect your adult child to make some financial contribution to the shared household.
- Keep on communicating. Don't let molehills become mountains.

QUESTIONS FOR YOU

1. Can you identify with Virginia's ambivalent feelings about having her son and daughter-in-law back home again?

2. What would you have done in her place?

3. If your own adult child were to come home tomorrow, would you take him/her in without hesitation?

4. How would it change your life?

5. What kind of contribution would you expect your adult child to make to the shared household?

6. Do you think there are times when an adult child should not be allowed to return home?

• 9 •

Battle Fatigue
Waiting Out the War

Some of us are like weary warriors, discouraged and battle-scarred in our quest for peace with one of our adult children. We may have wonderful rapport with one daughter and ongoing problems of communication with another. We may have experienced lifelong harmony in our relationship with one son and continual discord with another. If that is the case in your family, you have lots of company.

Many of us have learned the wisdom of standing back or standing by in situations where we are powerless to help, where help would be a hindrance, or where our involvement is considered intrusive. But waiting is hard. When our children take wrong turns, we want to put them back on track. When they suffer, we feel their pain.

There are situations that seem hopeless from our human perspective. Only faith in God's power to change lives keeps us from total despair as we watch a beloved child struggle against apparently impossible odds. How many of us have clung to the promise in Romans 8:28 that "in all things God works for the good of those who love him"?

In the last few months I've had an opportunity to watch a friend come into the light after twenty-two years of tunnel-darkness. Lorraine has given me permission to tell her story, hoping it will encourage the reader who is powerless to help an adult child in a desperate situation.

"I had an instinctive feeling that Tony was bad news the first time Carla brought him home," Lorraine said. "He was sullen, rude, and inconsiderate of our feelings *and* Carla's, even when he was supposed to be courting her. But she was nineteen and ready to assert her independence. The more Rob and I protested, which was probably a mistake, the more determined she was to marry him. When I saw that we weren't going to stop her, I tried to accept it and play mother-of-the-bride, but by that time she didn't want my help. She shut me out completely. Carla is our only daughter, and I'd always looked forward to the day she'd be married and all the stuff that goes along with planning a wedding. Her rejection was terribly hurtful, because we'd had so much fun doing 'girl' things together up until then.

"Rob and I tried to make friends with Tony—after all, he was our son-in-law—but every time we'd visit them in their apartment, he'd disappear. We got the message that he wasn't interested in any kind of relationship with us. Carla didn't encourage us to come over, either, so we only went when we had a reason, like taking something we thought they could use or delivering her birthday present. The very first year they were married, Tony forgot her birthday, and he just ignored occasions like Valentine's Day or Mother's Day— even with his own mother.

"I missed the close relationship Carla and I had had, but the thing that frustrated Rob the most was Tony's failure to hold a job. I think a lot of times they might have gone hungry without our care packages and loans from his mother. Tony's mother was a nice person. For the years before she died she kept trying to help them help themselves.

"Carla never told us anything about their finances, but we could see how poor they were by how run-down things got. Carla had always paid attention to her hair and makeup and she loved nice clothes, but after she was married she didn't seem to care much about how she looked. You know, that was really odd for a girl her age.

"We were almost relieved when they moved to another county. It was just too hard to watch her pulling away from us, and the worst of it was we didn't understand what was happening.

"After Carla's first baby came along, we visited the family more often. Tony continued to make himself scarce and Carla let us play the doting grandparents—as long as we didn't make too many suggestions. But we always came home more concerned than ever about the run-down condition of the house, the bald tires on the car, and the tense relationship between our daughter and her husband. Rob and I would talk far into the night about what we should or shouldn't do. When it came right down to it, we couldn't do very much of anything—except pray, and we did plenty of that."

Occasionally the situation would take a turn for the better. After Carla's second daughter was old enough for kindergarten, she found a part-time job.

"It gave her a new lease on life," Lorraine said. "She was getting out of the house again and meeting new people. And they finally had some health insurance! Things were looking up."

But a few months later the picture had changed again.

"Carla was talking about working full-time and finding an after-school sitter for the girls," Lorraine said. "Just when we thought she might be getting ready to leave Tony we heard she was pregnant again!"

Sometime later Lorraine got a call from a neighbor who said she'd taken Carla to the hospital for stitches. Tony had had too much champagne at a wedding and pushed Carla down when she tried to make him quit. Lorraine and Rob began to wonder if Tony had a drinking problem, on top of everything else. "Rob was wild," Lorraine said. "He finally got Tony on the phone and told him if he ever hurt Carla again he'd have us and the law to contend with."

Later, when we tried to call Carla to say we were coming down, the phone had been disconnected. We didn't know whether Tony pulled it out of the wall after he heard from Rob or if they couldn't pay the phone bill. We left breakfast dishes in the sink and headed south, praying all the way that God would protect our daughter. The drive seemed to take an eternity. When we arrived at Carla's, she was cool as could be. She told us that their neighbor had highly exaggerated her "accident," that she'd stumbled and fallen without any help from Tony. And they'd had a misunderstanding with the phone company over the bill, she said—no big deal.

Lorraine and Rob wanted to believe her. If Carla and Tony had come to the point where they couldn't pay their bills, what were they to do? They couldn't afford to support two families on a retirement income. They were already bringing in groceries and trying to keep the kids in shoes and school clothes, but if they started paying the utility bills, wouldn't they just be prolonging the inevitable? Though Lorraine knew divorce wasn't God's best plan, she began to pray that Carla would finally get fed up and leave "that bum."

Over the following months Tony became more abusive than ever. When he drank he flew into rages and broke things. Once he pushed a heavy chair through the living room window; another time he threw Carla's clothes on the lawn and doused them with bleach. One night he spray-painted the word "PIG" on the house of the young policeman who lived next door.

Some of these incidents didn't come out until later, but Lorraine and Rob heard enough to be concerned for the safety of their grandchildren. They sought advice from the local family service agency.

"Please understand," said the woman behind the desk. "If you tell me your grandchildren are either abused or neglected, it's my responsibility to remove them from their home."

"We just couldn't do that," Lorraine said. "We'd lose touch with our daughter altogether if we had her children taken away from her. Carla had always been a loving mother, even though she couldn't seem to free herself from the destructive relationship she was in. She was still holding us at arm's length, so there was a lot we didn't know. If we'd known then she was a battered wife we might have been able to get her into a shelter somewhere. We *did* consider the idea of bringing the children to live with us, but that's a pretty awesome prospect at our ages. Of course, if we'd known how bad things were . . ."

Carla finally filed for divorce on her eighteenth anniversay, but the story continued. Because Tony had no money, no job, and nowhere to turn, the judge, with Carla's assent, allowed him to remain in the family home—sleeping in a converted corner of the garage.

Lorraine and Rob applauded the strength their daughter had shown in breaking free of her marriage. "We knew it took a lot of courage for her to take such a big step," Lorraine said. "Still, things didn't change much. We went down to visit a little more often, but we found it hard to be encouraging when there was so much we disapproved of—especially Tony hanging around. And there was such clutter and confusion. Carla grew up in a neat and tidy house. I couldn't understand her letting things go like that. But we couldn't say anything without her getting on the defensive. We walked on eggs most of the time."

Tony was supposed to pay child support, but there was never anything left over from what little he made doing odd jobs. Carla found a day-care provider for the baby and went back to work. Her parents were encouraged that she seemed to be getting her life together when she broke her hand in another "accident."

"She said she got in between Tony and his brother when

they got in a fight over their mother's will. Carla's mother-in-law was fairly well off, but she left most of Tony's share of her estate in trust for his kids. Believe it or not, she named *me* as trustee. She knew I'd look out for our grandchildren. She probably anticipated Tony's angry reaction. The poor woman agonized as much over her son as we did over Carla.

"Things hit a new low last November. Rob and I stopped at Carla's on our way to spend the Thanksgiving holiday with friends in Arizona. The gas had been shut off, so there was no heat and no hot water for baths or dishes. And there was *no* food in the house! Needless to say, we gathered everyone up and took them out to eat and then shopping for supplies, including a big turkey and all the trimmings. The kids had a ball, dancing down the aisles and picking out goodies for their dinner. Before we left town we stopped at the Harbor Inn and made reservations for Christmas."

Lorraine and Rob reserved a suite for three days over Christmas—a living room with a fireplace, beds to sleep six, and a fully equipped kitchen. They brought a small Christmas tree and decorations from home. On Christmas Eve Carla and the children came to sing carols and sip hot cider in front of the fire, and on Christmas morning the children awoke to presents heaped around the tree.

"For the first time in years we felt like family," Lorraine said. "Rob and I came home with renewed hope."

Proverbs 13:12 says, "Hope deferred makes the heart sick." Lorraine experienced the truth of that Scripture when her hope was deferred yet again. Just a few weeks after their holiday celebration, Lorraine and Rob received a call telling them that Tony had tried to kill Carla. The screams of the frightened children and the quick response of the young policeman next door had saved her life. Carla was determined that this would be the last time Tony abused her.

With Tony in jail on the assault charge and Carla ready to sever her last ties to him, Lorraine and Rob were able to help their daughter begin to heal physically, emotionally, and spiritually. Last week they helped Carla move to a small town just a short drive from their home. The money left in trust for the children was put to good use—as a down payment on a new home and a new beginning for them.

"Our lawyer advised us that we could invest part of Tony's mother's money in real estate. Talk about things working together for good! The children love the local school and Carla has good prospects for a job. She looks like a different person—like the daughter we thought we'd lost. She goes around smiling and hugging herself all the time! They're all getting counseling, too, so I know they'll come out of this okay. I have nothing but optimism about the future."

This has been a long story about a long night of waiting and praying for change in a desperate situation. When Carla made an unfortunate choice of marriage partners, her parents were destined to share her suffering in the years to come. The dark years eventually ended, but many similar stories fail to end as happily.

Perhaps you're waiting out a battle of your own, hoping, praying that a child will find peace—with God, with you, with other significant people, and with himself or herself. From your human viewpoint, progress in your son's or daughter's life seems to take forever. I know. I've felt that way sometimes. But God has encouraged me over the years.

Remember the night I lay awake fretting (ignoring all the "do not fret" verses in Psalms and Proverbs!) about our newly emancipated children? Hindsight shows me that God used the worrisome circumstances that surrounded each young adult then to help them grow into the confident, mature men and women they are today. They are still growing, of course, and I am still on my knees with an impatient heart. But God reminds me that his refining operation is a lifelong process.

At one point or another all parents of adult children are prone to battle fatigue (or callouses on our knees!). We wait and pray for a miracle that will free our children from destructive relationships, crippling addictions, or whatever else may be robbing their lives of joy. We would gladly trade places with them on the front lines, but the battle is theirs. As allies we can demonstrate our love by standing by, ready to help as God leads.

And we can remember the promise in Psalm 30:5:

> For his anger lasts only a moment,
>   but his favor lasts a lifetime
> Weeping may remain for a night,
>   but rejoicing comes in the morning.

QUESTIONS FOR YOU

1. What "waiting and praying" situation in your life helps you identify with Lorraine and Rob?

2. When, if ever, have you been hurt or disappointed by an adult child's rejection?

3. What do you think you would do if you suspected your adult child was in an abusive relationship?

4. How do you feel about the ways that Lorraine and Rob chose to help their daughter?

5. Do you think they did enough? Too much? Explain.

6. Given the same circumstances, would you have paid Carla's utility bills? Why or why not?

7. What role do you think grandparents should play in a situation such as Carla's?

· 10 ·

Ambassador for Peace
Continuing Harmony Between Generations

By the time we have come to be parents of adult children, we have lived at least half our lives. We are different people in our fifties and sixties than we were in our twenties and thirties—those active parenting days that in many ways carved the future for our young adults of today. We have gained insight born of our hindsight and wisdom born of our experience. Too late, some of us sigh, to do it over and do it better.

If we are grandparents, we look at our grandchildren and see freshness and beauty that sometimes, for the parent, hides behind smudged faces, runny noses, and mismatched outfits. Our children were like that, we remember, and we were as nearsighted as the parents of our grandchildren. Farsightedness came with age! We long to recapture what too often escaped us, weighed down as we were by our cloaks of responsibility and our goals of perfection.

I speak for myself here, but I suspect that every parent of grandparent age feels at least an occasional twinge of nostalgic regret over years that seemed—in retrospect—to be set on fast-forward. Human beings, unlike animals, are gifted with memories that can bring both smiles and tears. But

God's word would remind us that we cannot plow today's field while looking over our shoulders at yesterday (Luke 9:62). To focus on missed opportunities of the past is counterproductive. We have today at our disposal and fresh new opportunities to build satisfying relationships with our adult children.

REASSIGNMENT

We parents of adult children have already recognized our need to accept a new place in the family system. Where once, by right of seniority, we had automatic authority over our younger generation, the years have reassigned us to a rear-guard position. The passage of time continually changes the balance and structure of our family network. Whatever else may have happened over the years to alter circumstances and relationships within our extended families, we as parents will be challenged to remain flexible. Continuing harmony between generations will depend upon our willingness to swim with the tide.

While the earlier adjustment from head of the nuclear family to center of the extended family is usually more rewarding than sacrificial, the succeeding moves are less predictable and more difficult for most of us. We may feel at times as if we are only fringe members of what used to be our undisputed domain. Is our grip on the edge of the family circle as precarious as it sometimes feels? Are we destined to be gently pushed into exile from the lives of the ones we've loved beyond expression?

Our nagging fears are magnified in the wee hours of the morning when we lie awake wondering about a son's lack of communication or a daughter's failure to include us in her holiday plans. A letter, a phone call, or an invitation to lunch reassures us and wipes away cowardly visions of lonely nursing homes; a holiday weekend with the grandchildren sends us home with renewed appreciation for our quiet space.

As we grow older, many of us dread the threat of financial or physical dependence that so often comes in the declining years, especially to the widowed or divorced who live alone. We—once the "givers" in our relationships with the younger generation—recoil at the thought of role reversal in our old age. We want our children to include us in their lives because our presence somehow enriches those lives, not because they are obligated to care for us. We want to keep a significant place in the family network. We want to *belong* as we have in previous years.

Everyone, young or old, needs a feeling of belonging—a place where we fit into the scheme of things. In our postparenting years that need can be at least partially satisfied in many areas: through a strong marital relationship, through participation in community and church groups, through close friendships. But if we lose our "place" with our adult children, we are bound to feel a void in our lives.

If we rely primarily on our adult children for emotional support, we are bound to feel threatened by the natural distancing that comes as they are more and more involved with their nuclear families. We may respond to the widening generation gap in various ways: we may fight to maintain the status quo, we may succumb to self-pity, or we may be prodded to further growth in other areas of our lives.

NEW HORIZONS

The basket beside my living room chair is heaped to overflowing with invitations for adventure.

- The latest schedule of classes from our local junior college contains both credit courses and adult education opportunities.

- The *Elderhostel Catalog* announces its International Program with tantalizing offers to explore far-away places. Photos show participants planting trees in Jerusalem, confronting kangaroos in Australia, and dancing with schoolchildren in the former Soviet Union.

● This week's *Santa Ynez Valley News* features articles about a new class in short story writing, a reception and show for a local artist, and a Western Dance class at Veteran's Memorial Hall.

● Underneath those items are the library books and current magazines I haven't had time to read. Clear at the bottom of the basket is a piece of needlework I began last year!

If I am ever bored, it won't be from a lack of things to do!

At forty-seven I might have been content to watch soap operas and knit little things for that season's crop of grandchildren. But somewhere someone prayed for me and the Hound of Heaven was on my trail.

I went—without enthusiasm—to a nondenominational Bible study for women and was catapulted into new life. The spiritual awakening that came to me as I began the fascinating study of the Bible expanded my horizons in every direction. I began to change in my response to life's experiences.

Before my conversion, a diagnosis of breast cancer might have seemed like the end of the world. Now, with the Lord as my Shepherd, I found unaccustomed strength. Courage and serenity, the supernatural by-products of my new faith, sustained me through the trauma of radical surgery and followed me through many months of radiation and chemo-therapy. I learned what it was to be "struck down but not destroyed." Harry saw something different in me and was drawn to look more closely at the Source. As my new friends in the Christian community ministered to us with casseroles and prayers, God drew my husband into the faith that we've shared for nearly twenty years.

My first "horizon," then, was a spiritual one that enriched and tightened our marital bond like nothing else

ever could have. Like every other second-time-arou~~~
~~~riage, ours had come from a background of pain and ~
tragedy. By the grace of God and in spite of our emotiona~
scars, our love had managed to survive the first dozen years of
our blended family. When Harry and I came to know Christ
in a personal way and gradually made him Lord of our lives,
our marriage took on a new dimension. I count our mutual
rebirth as a precious gift from God. It's the element of
stability in our continually evolving relationship with each
other and with our children and grandchildren.

Recovery from my life-threatening illness gave me a new
appreciation for living and learning. We moved to an empty-
nest house with a studio and I tried my hand at oil painting. I
not only learned a craft, but I found friends I never would
have known otherwise. Although I've suspended painting to
concentrate on writing, the awareness of shapes and colors
has forever changed my way of looking at the world around
me.

Harry and I together have dabbled in the study of
subjects from genealogy to desert creepy crawlies. We've
explored the United States by motorhome and walked in the
footsteps of Jesus in Israel. At home, we have hobbies we
pursue separately that make our time together more interesting.

The point is, in order to keep from leaning too heavily on
our adult children, we have found interests and activities
outside our parenthood roles—new horizons. We may be
limited in our choices by the state of our budget or health, but
there is an opportunity or a need in our community to fit each
of us.

Your role may be predetermined by necessity—an
obligation to an elderly parent or responsiblity for the care of
a grandchild—or you may have the freedom to choose from a
wide range of interests. Those of us who have a life partner,
good health, sufficient money to pay our bills, and enough

time for a new adventure are fortunate, but even without these things we can find a focus for independent living.

SHARING RESOURCES

Independence does not mean that we must stop giving to our children from our store of resources, although our material resources may diminish as we grow older. If we are to be comfortable with that fact, we will need to see the value of the spiritual gifts we can bring to our relationships.

When Maureen and Stan's three children were in the process of establishing their own homes and families, Stan was at the earning peak of his career and able to help the young people with down payments on their houses and other material needs.

"It was our pleasure to help the kids," Maureen said. "It was partly selfish, of course, because it kept us involved in their lives when they might have chosen to be more independent. In the last few years, though, our financial status has changed drastically. Last year we were straining our retirement budget to send the usual birthday checks to our eight grandchildren."

"Our children might not understand our position," Stan said, "but I hope they don't think we care any less about them. Even if they do, I'm not about to make excuses for the change in our lifestyle. The kids are pretty well set now in their own right, and I think my first responsibility is to provide for our old age so we won't have to be dependent on them."

Many of us find ourselves in a similar position as we reach retirement age. We may have delighted in showering our children with material gifts when we were able. But if material giving has been the primary evidence of our love for our children, a sudden decrease in our gifts may be misunderstood. We can guard against that possibility by learning to demonstrate our love in other ways.

We can give of our time and energy. My friend Helen devised a creative solution to changing circumstances. "My son lives a hundred miles away. He and his wife are both so busy that we can't rely on them to make contact with us. We used to go up and stay in a motel and take them out for dinner, which gave us a chance to visit and fit in with their crowded schedule. But that got to be pretty expensive, so we've had to figure out something else or settle for seeing them less often. My latest strategy is to call and ask, 'Can we come to dinner one night this week if we bring the dinner?' Then we go early enough to head for home by eight o'clock. It takes a day out of our lives to see them for a few hours, but we're at the stage of having more time than money."

When health and energy are high, you can meet some obvious needs in the lives of your adult children. You can take the grandchildren for a weekend, help with a spring cleaning project, or volunteer to pinch-hit for a busy parent at 4-H Exhibit Day.

We can give of our attention. We can show interest in the interests of our young adults and concern for their concerns. As long as our minds continue to function, we can pray for our children. We can read between the lines of letters or listen between the words of conversations to hear unexpressed needs. We can look for ways to reassure and encourage, even though there are times they may not hear us. Where God declines to use us in a position of leadership, he will use our prayers.

In considering the things you can do for your adult children, know that *doing* is not the primary function of parenthood. You will always want to *do* something to help your children dodge bullets and avoid booby traps on their life's journey. We have a natural urge to continue the task we began when we assumed the duties of parenting. But remember that God's assignment for us was to provide the basic training for our children and let him take over leadership on the battlefield.

Authors Arthur Maslow and Moira Duggan make our rear-echelon positions clear:

> With our grown children, the measure of how well we're doing is more in the *lack* of parenting than in any active role we may take. As parents of adults, we need to let go of responsibility toward our children and let them find their own path instead. Whereas before we were responsible for *doing*, now we are responsible for *being*. Whereas before we were providers and advisors, now we can be storytellers and fountains of experience. We can and should be available to listen and to give advice when asked—but only when asked. Whether what we know out of our experience is true or false is not the point. The point is that we share what we know with our children. That, I believe, is the magic we can give to them once they are grown.[1]

As God leads, tell your stories and share your experience. He will use them as tools in shaping and molding your adult children. The qualities you demonstrate will have an impact on your children's lives long after you are gone.

In a previous chapter we saw the value of modeling flexibility, enthusiasm, and faith as we continue to grow in our later years. We explored the opportunities for affecting our children's lives through our love and influence. Those opportunities will continue for our lifetime.

AREAS OF CONFLICT

Having established a relatively independent life of our own, open to personal growth and new experience, we are in a better position to maintain good peer relationships with our adult children. They can be our greatest allies and friends, as long as we don't demand that they be our *only* friends. Vicki, a young acquaintance, gave me her perspective of this common area of conflict between parents and their adult children.

"My mother is always complaining that I don't spend

enough time with her," Vicki said. "I'm sorry, but I'm absolutely drowning in obligations to my kids and my husband and my job. I feel guilty enough that I'm not doing as much as I should in any of those departments, and I don't need Mother to lay another guilt trip on me. She still drives, so there are lots of things she could do to fill her time. If she wants to see more of her grandchildren, she could take some of the pressure off of me by running them around to their soccer games and piano lessons."

Now, there's an idea. When we're feeling left out of our adult child's life, we can look for a place we can be of help and offer our services. That's what good friends do for each other.

In every intergenerational relationship there are areas of conflict. Here are others that may disturb the peace in your family:

The child-raising issues. Where the infant grandchildren once brought us closer to our young adult children, adolescent grandchildren may contribute to the generation gap between us. Ann explained why she finds it difficult to have her parents around her teenaged son.

"Don and I have enough battles over Taylor and his grades and his driving privileges without my parents' advice on how to handle a sixteen-year-old. When we're having one of our family squabbles, I dread seeing my mom and dad come around. They really don't understand the kids of today, and they're apt to get off on Taylor's latest hair style or something equally irrelevant. They just add more friction to a tense situation."

Most of us respect our children's need for privacy within their families and have no desire to share in the everyday care and discipline of our grandchildren. Even so, we can't resist an occasional opportunity to express the values we uphold, hoping our grandchildren will absorb our standards for living and stay out of harm's way.

Grandparents are naturally concerned about how their

grandchildren are being raised. We have made mistakes in our parenting that we regret, and we want to warn our children away from the same pitfalls. We have learned a few things, too, and we want to pass on the benefits of our experience. My experience—and input from the younger generation—tells me we need to tread very softly here.

Our children need encouragement, not criticism, as they work through their own parenting problems. If we find ourselves involved in the dynamics of our young families, we can give positive reinforcement—sincere praise of things well done—instead of unsolicited advice. Our children will not do things the way we would (or *think* we would), but we are wise to keep our suggestions to a minimum. Except in cases of neglect or abuse, our children's parenting methods are their concern, not ours.

The financial issues. Each nuclear family has a different style of handling money. This is another area that can cause conflict between adult children and their parents. Bill and his wife buy a new car every two years and vacation in Hawaii—"None of our business," say his parents, "except that he still owes us five thousand dollars from four years ago." Parents tire of dependent or wasteful children and drive around with bumper stickers that say: "WE'RE SPENDING OUR KIDS' INHERITANCE." One "kid" told me that he was offended by the rejection implicit in that message. He reminds me that we should show enough respect for adult children to be straightforward with them about our circumstances and intentions.

Young adults often question their elders' wisdom or competence in handling their financial affairs. Ramona hears from an aunt that her elderly father withdrew half his life savings to bail her brother out of debt. "It's my dad's money," she says, "but he's getting a little forgetful. I think Bud is taking advantage of him." If Ramona's relationship with her father is sound, she should be able to express her concern to him directly.

The family-tradition issues. Many a war has been waged over who will go where on which holiday. Maybe your family has *always* gone to Grandma's the weekend before Christmas to string cranberries and popcorn balls. But your new son-in-law, Justin, insists on spoiling everything by scheduling a get-together with his parents that weekend. Your daughter Cheryl isn't putting up much protest, and her siblings are all mad at her. As parents, you're caught in the middle of what threatens to become a family feud.

Family traditions are wonderful, but they must remain subject to change, or even cancellation, as the family changes. Traditions are not more important than the individuals involved.

The divorced-parents issues. Because of our generation's rate of marriage failure (forty percent of people in their twenties have divorced parents, according to statistics), many of our young adults have two sets of parents. Jealousy flares when Mary chooses to spend her week of vacation with her father and stepmother instead of with you. Other emotions arise when you hear she's deliberately avoiding the stepsibling that came with your remarriage. Adult children tell me they feel torn between loyalties and find it hard to fairly divide their time and attention between parents. We can be generous enough to make it easier for them.

The family-grapevine issues. One of the most common causes of conflict between family members is the molehill that becomes a mountain as it travels the family grapevine. "Sally said that Mom said that you said . . ." Because we are family, we assume the privilege of talking about one another. We share information, sometimes indiscriminately, about one member to another. But second- and third-party reporting is almost always inaccurate and often destructive to fragile relationships within the family. We need to use discernment when talking to each other *about* each other.

You will find that each of these common problems have

their gray areas. There are no hard and fast rules about dealing with the issues of finances, grandchildren, or traditions. But try to recognize and handle with care the issues in your own family that may create dissension among your members.

A friend who has overcome obstacles to achieve an unusually close relationship with her adult children shared her formula for success:

Tell what you need.

Say how you feel.

Let the other person respond as he will.

If I wish my son would keep in closer contact with me, I had better tell him so. Otherwise I run the risk of harboring resentment which will inevitably come out in bursts of anger, spurts of sarcasm, or periods of silence. I find I can be honest without being accusatory ("*I* need you in my life," rather than "*You* don't come around often enough.")

Where human relationships are involved, occasional conflict is inevitable. If hostilities arise between family members, we can choose our allies and take up arms or we can be ambassadors for peace, promoting compassion and understanding between hostile camps.

PEACE TALKS

According to the sociologists, members of the older generation put a high priority on keeping peace. The older we are and the more we realize our time is growing short, the greater value we place on our family relationships. We become more cautious about sensitive issues, to the extent that we may abandon discussion of every serious subject in favor of safe small talk.

One middle-aged son expressed his disappointment at the lack of serious communication between him and his elderly parents. "These intelligent, aware older adults seem hesitant to explore and voice their opinions," he says. His parents, like many of us, are probably tiptoeing around a number of thorny issues, trying to keep the family get-togethers peaceful and pleasant. Sociologists find that the natural tendency to become more outspoken with age is usually counteracted by a desire to avoid family conflict.

In any long-standing relationship, especially one that exists within the framework of a complex family system, misunderstandings and occasional clashes are unavoidable. If we are naturally peace-at-any-price personalities, we may back away from any confrontation. We will choose to defuse any explosive situation by pacifying the agressors, suppressing our own feelings, and avoiding in the future whatever issue caused the conflict. Suppressed feelings, however, affect our attitudes and inhibit our future relationship with the person we failed to confront.

In expressing anger, hurt, or fear, we run the risk of escalating a skirmish into a battle; but if unspoken feelings cause us to erect barriers, the price of our silence is too high. Resolving misunderstandings as they arise will prevent the family molehills from becoming mountains.

Monica learned that truth in dealing with her daughter-in-law. "Kelly could be sweet as pie," she says, "but when she'd get mad at Barry over something, she'd make snide remarks about how his sisters and I spoiled him and how she had to go to all the work of retraining him. She protected herself by saying it in a joking way, but I got the message loud and clear. It made me furious. I guess what bothered me was that there's more than a grain of truth in her accusation, but it was unkind of her to rub it in.

"I didn't want to take a chance of alienating my son by fighting with his wife," Monica continued, "but as long as I let it slide, her words ate at me for days afterwards. Then I'd blow up at her about some totally unrelated thing and Barry would get dragged into it anyway. I found it was better to let Kelly know how her 'kidding' remarks made me feel, even though it took some pride-swallowing to do it. I think Kelly's and my personalities will always clash some, but it's important to me to have a good relationship with her because of Barry. I think we've made some progress in understanding each other."

We can't have good relationships without understanding, and we can only understand each other through honest communication.

> Family counselors and other mental health professionals agree that frequent and meaningful communication between all family members is crucial for resolving issues, heading off destructive confrontations, and reinforcing family unity. Without open conversation, a family's growth can be stunted by resentment, conflict, and passivity.[2]

NECESSARY NOURISHMENT

Communication, the lifeblood of every relationship, is by far the most important element in maintaining strong ties between family members.

The wall above my desk is covered with portraits and snapshots of people I love. The pictures represent milestones of our family life—graduations, weddings, and reunions. Two-dimensional images recall flesh-and-blood people and the love relationships I've had with each of them. They stir up cherished memories, but memories cannot carry a relationship. My bond with the son or daughter who smiles down on me is nourished by our communication—by letters and telephone calls and the tingle of anticipation that comes with "See you soon, Mom!"

A portrait of my late father and another of a little boy who died forty years ago bring nostalgic smiles and tears to my heart, but they don't restore relationship. Communication with Dad and my son was cut off by death and our relationship is suspended—this side of heaven.

Relationships with our adult children can survive a

necessary separation, but without communication to bridge the distance between us, they will dry up like tender plants deprived of food and water. Our relationships are fragile. Some, grown in a controlled environment, flourish like hothouse plants. Others, rooted in rocky soil or exposed to harsh climate, need constant nurturing to keep them alive. Some of our relationships have been late bloomers, responding to the pruning of dead wood of the past. Each relationship is a unique treasure, worthy of the nourishment of honest communication.

Honest communication means speaking the truth in love. Truth is the protective armor of our love relationships. Without truth, deceit and distrust can invade and infect our most intimate bonds. Without truth, love cannot thrive, understanding cannot grow, and respect has no foothold. Truth demands courageous honesty and humble transparency. It calls for looking inward to self-knowledge and reaching outward with self-sharing. It is communication without subterfuge or secrecy. This is not to deny the areas of privacy in our lives, for parents and children alike have a right to healthy independence. Honest communication has to do with integrity in our relationships.

AN INSTRUMENT OF PEACE

There is an advantage to the perspective we achieve as we withdraw from front-line interaction with our grown children. It is easier now, from the distance across our current generation gap, to see the divisive elements in our strained relationships and work toward peace where there has been discord. Perhaps we have the perfect opportunity to align our goals with those of the familiar prayer attributed to Saint Francis of Assisi:

> Lord, make me an instrument of Your peace. Where there is hatred let me sow love; where there is injury, pardon; where there is doubt, faith; where there is

despair, hope; where there is darkness, light; and where there is sadness, joy.

O divine Master, grant that I may not so much seek to be consoled as to console; to be understood as to understand; to be loved as to love. For it is in giving that we receive; it is in pardoning that we are pardoned; and it is in dying that we are born to eternal life.

What better place to apply that powerful prayer than to our relationships with our adult children. We can be an instrument of God's peace, not backing away from every threat of conflict, but working within the web of relationships in our extended family. As parents of adults who are fighting their personal battles on life's front lines, we have an opportunity to be God's ambassadors, giving gifts of reconciliation from our rear-echelon posts.

Where there is hatred . . . Hate is love turned inside out. Although we may resist using such a harsh word in connection with a family member, hate is precisely the emotion we feel when we are hurt or rejected by someone who is supposed to love us. It is the prideful, defensive, self-protective response to a withdrawal of love by someone we trusted. It is anger, self-pity, and resentment. It hurts the giver at least as much as it hurts the recipient. It negates the potential for joy from every relationship.

Love—the essence of God—is the antidote for hatred. "Love one another" is a clear directive. Look for ways to "sow" love in your difficult family relationships.

Where there is injury . . . The closer our relationships, the more vulnerable we are. Once wounded by another's anger or rejection, we can choose one of two paths: to retaliate in attitude or action or to pardon the one who hurt us. The words "Forgive us our trespasses as we forgive" show us what our choice should be.

I like what Gordon MacDonald says about forgiveness:

Forgiveness just might be the keystone in the arch of all relationships where loving and being loved is an issue.

The failure to give or receive forgiveness probably accounts for the collapse of marriages, families and friendships.

To forgive is to withhold judgment, forswear vengeance, renounce bitterness, break the silence of estrangement, to actually wish the best for the person who has hurt us.[3]

Where there is doubt, despair, darkness, sadness . . . We suffer when one of our children suffers, whether he is four or forty.

● Moira's heart aches for a daughter whose husband has left her for another woman.

● Derek watches helplessly as his son faces bankruptcy and the loss of his business.

● Patricia grieves for children who have turned their backs on Christian values and are leading immoral lives.

If we are Christians and our children are not, we long to bring them the kind of comfort we have found in our own faith. But faith is a gift from God, not from parents, and the despair our child may feel in his personal hour of darkness may be the key that opens his heart to the message of the gospel.

As parents of adults who are beyond our authority, our part is to pray that they will find peace in recognizing the authority of God. We can be his instruments, as Saint Francis says, sharing our hope as we encourage our adult children in their seemingly hopeless situations. In looking to God for our own strength and wisdom, we will reflect that divine light and dispel some of the darkness in our child's life. We know the joy that lives in our hearts despite the circumstances of the moment, and although we can't give it away, we can demonstrate its power as we interact with our families. We can sow the seeds of God's peace and trust Him for the harvest.

QUESTIONS FOR YOU

1. In what ways has the balance and structure of your family network changed over the years?

2. How have you seen your position in the family system change with the changing circumstances?

3. What things in your life give you a feeling of "belonging"?

4. In what areas can you find opportunities for personal growth and new experience outside your family?

5. What new ways are you finding to fit into your adult children's lives?

6. Think about the openness of communication between you and each of your adult children. Do you see a correlation between the amount of openness and the depth of relationship?

7. What particular areas of conflict have you identified within your family? How have you dealt with conflict involving your adult children?

8. In what ways can you be "an instrument for peace" within your family?

• Notes •

2 – Declaration of War

[1]Jay Kesler, *Ten Mistakes Parents Make with Teenagers (And How to Avoid Them)* (Brentwood, Tennessee: Wolgemeth and Hyatt Publishers, Inc., 1988), 19.

3 – Standing Watch

[1]Dr. Jeffrey Rubin and Dr. Carol Rubin, *When Families Fight: How to Handle Conflict with Those You Love* (New York: William Morrow, Inc., 1989), 227.

4 – Cease-Fire

[1]Judith Viorst, *Necessary Losses* (New York: Simon and Schuster, 1986), 230.
[2]Merrill C. Tenney, General Editor, *The Zondervan Pictorial Bible Dictionary* (Grand Rapids: Zondervan Publishing House, 1963), 632.

5 – Old Wounds

[1]Melinda Blau, "Adult Children Tied to the Past," *American Health* (July-August 1990): 60.
[2]Ann Landers, *Santa Barbara News-Press*, 27 August 1990, D3.
[3]Landers, *Santa Barbara News-Press*, 21 May 1990, D5.

6 – Reconnaissance

[1]Rubin, *When Families Fight*, 245.
[2]Gail Sheehy, *Pathfinders* (New York: William Morrow and Co., Inc. 1981), 220.

[3]Sheehy, *Pathfinders*, 228.

[4]Harold Ivan Smith, *You and Your Parents: Strategies for Building an Adult Relationship* (Minneapolis: Augsburg Publishing House, 1987), 40.

[5]Jerry and Mary White, *When Your Kids Aren't Kids Anymore: Parenting Late-Teen and Adult Children* (Colorado Springs: Navpress, 1989), 42–43.

[6]C. S. Lewis, *The Four Loves* (New York: Harcourt Brace Jovanovich, 1960), 53.

[8]Arthur Maslow, M.S.W., and Moira Duggan, *Family Connections: Parenting Your Grown Children* (New York: Doubleday and Co., Inc., 1982), 75.

7 – Selective Service

[1]Carolyn Johnson, *Understanding Alcoholism: Answers to Questions People Ask* (Grand Rapids: Zondervan, 1991).

[2]"Detachment," a statement based on Al-Anon's conference-approved literature (New York: Al-Anon Family Group Headquarters, Inc., 1981).

8 – Recalled to Active Duty

[1]Helen Hosier, *You Never Stop Being a Parent* (Old Tappan, N.J.: Revell, 1986).

10 – Ambassador for Peace

[1]Maslow and Duggan, *Family Connections*, 79.

[2]Don Gabor, *How to Talk to the People You Love* (New York: Simon and Schuster, Inc., 1989), 164.

[3]Gordon MacDonald, "How to Experience Forgiveness from the Heart," *Christian Herald* (March/April 1991): 18.